14 Days

OCT 3 1 1935
NOV 2 3 1935
JAN 2 5 1936
FEB 2 0 1936
MAY 4   1936
JUL 1 4 1936
JL 21 36
JUL 2 4 1936
AUG 2 2 1936
JAN 5 '09

W9-AXC-155

WITHDRAWN

THE OLD MAID

DRAMATIZED BY ZOË AKINS
from the Novel by
EDITH WHARTON

As produced at the Empire Theatre in New York, "The Old Maid" has proved one of the most distinguished dramatic successes that have graced the recent American stage. And there are reasons for this. There is the fine, poignant, sensitive novel by Edith Wharton upon which Miss Akins' play has been based. Then, there is the superb and finished dramatization by a foremost American playwright. And finally, in the New York production, the highest praise is due for the inspired performances in the leading roles, of Judith Anderson and Helen Menken, and for the excellent directing of Guthrie McClintic.

The scene of the play is Old New York where a firmly entrenched society holds sway. The period, covered by five episodes, spans from the 1830's to the 1850's. How firmly rooted in stiff, arid formalities of conduct was this society is indicated by the manner in which Charlotte Lovell's misstep was hidden in a world that was so compactly knit. But hidden it was, and this remarkable drama takes one behind the scenes to the innermost recesses of the hearts of two women. You will follow with rapt attention the subtle disclosure of the fate of Charlotte Lovell, as her true role of mother is assumed by her cousin, Delia Ralston, and the play sweeps to its ironic end. "The Old Maid" is unreservedly commended for its actable quality. It also makes reading of a most absorbing kind.

THE OLD MAID

*Dramatized by Zoë Akins
from the novel by
Edith Wharton*

D. APPLETON-CENTURY COMPANY
INCORPORATED
NEW YORK   1935   LONDON

COPYRIGHT, 1934, 1935, BY EDITH WHARTON AND ZOË AKINS

All rights reserved. This book, or parts thereof, must not be reproduced in any form without permission of the publisher.

WARNING

. The fact that you have purchased this copy of THE OLD MAID does not give you permission to produce it, or to give public readings of it, unless you have received permission to do so.

This play is fully protected in all countries by the copyright law, all requirements of which have been complied with. No performance, professional or amateur, no public reading, no radio broadcast, may be given without permission of the publishers, D. Appleton-Century Co., Inc., 35 West 32nd Street, New York City, and 34 Bedford Street, Covent Garden, London, or of Alice Kauser, 152 West 42nd Street, New York City, agent for the author.

Performances of this play are subject to royalty. Any one presenting this play without the consent of the publishers or the author's agent, will be liable to the penalties provided by law.

"Section 4966—Any person publicly performing or representing any dramatic or musical composition for which copyright has been obtained, without the consent of the proprietor of said dramatic or musical composition, or his heirs and assigns, shall be liable for damages, in all cases, to be assessed at such sum, not less than one hundred dollars for the first and fifty dollars for every subsequent performance, as to the court shall appear just. If the unlawful performance and presentation be willful and for profit, such person or persons shall be imprisoned for a period not exceeding one year." U. S. Revised Statutes: Title 60, Chapter 3.

Copyright, 1924, by D. Appleton and Company
Copyright, 1922, by The Consolidated Magazines Corporation
(The Red Book Magazine)

PRINTED IN THE UNITED STATES OF AMERICA

THE OLD MAID

THE OLD MAID was produced at the Empire Theatre, New York, on January 7, 1935, under the management of Harry Moses, and the artistic direction of Guthrie McClintic, with the following actors in the important rôles:

DELIA LOVELL.....................*Judith Anderson*

CHARLOTTE LOVELL.................*Helen Menken*

DR. LANSKELL......................*George Nash*

MRS. MINGOTT.....................*Margaret Dale*

CLEMENTINA ....*Margaret Anderson*

JAMES RALSTON....................*Frederic Voight*

JOSEPH RALSTON...................*Robert Wallsten*

LANNING HALSEY ....*John Cromwell*

JOHN HALSEY ....*Warren Trent*

DELIA HALSEY ....*Florence Williams*

NORA..................................*Dona Earl*

MRS. JENNIE MEADE..................*Mary Ricard*

TINA (at age of 5)..................*Yvonne Mann*

SUSAN..............................*Gloria Mann*

TOMMY............................*Jackie Grimes*

BENNY........................*Charles Wiley, Jr.*

BRIDGET............................*Hope Landin*

SERVANT............................*Gail Reade*

THE OLD MAID

The scene is the city of New York, and the action begins in the 'Thirties of the last century and continues through five episodes into the 'Fifties.

FIRST EPISODE

1833 DELIA LOVELL'S *room in her parents' country house, Lovell Place, at Avenue A and Ninety-first Street, overlooking the East River.*

SECOND EPISODE

1839 CHARLOTTE LOVELL'S *day-nursery in a room above the* LOVELL *stables in the rear of her grandmother's house in Mercer Street.*

THIRD EPISODE

1839 *The* JAMES RALSTONS' *drawing-room in their house in Gramercy Park; that same evening after dinner.*

FOURTH EPISODE

1853 *The same drawing-room; an evening in December.*

FIFTH EPISODE

1854 *The same; an evening the following June.*

NOTE: In the production at the Empire Theatre, the intermissions were after the second and third episodes.

CHARACTERS

DELIA LOVELL (afterwards Mrs. James Ralston)

CHARLOTTE LOVELL (Chatty)

DR. LANSKELL

MRS. MINGOTT

JAMES RALSTON

JOSEPH RALSTON

CLEMENTINA (Tina)

LANNING HALSEY

JOHN HALSEY

DELIA HALSEY (Dee)

NORA

JENNIE MEADE

BRIDGET

A SERVANT

SEVERAL CHILDREN

FIRST EPISODE

1833

Ten minutes before the hour set for Delia Lovell's
marriage, on a day in June.

Delia *is looking at herself in the mirror of her
dressing-table, while* Nora, *her maid, arranges
the orange-blossoms in her Brussels veil. She
wears a high-waisted "India mull," embroidered
with daisies, and white satin sandals. She is perfectly calm, although the string orchestra now
playing a selection from Gluck in the passage outside the long drawing-room downstairs will soon
change to the wedding march, and a knock on the
door will tell her that her father and her brides-
maids are waiting at the head of the stairs. But*
Nora *is not calm, and when she speaks there is
just a suggestion of disappointment in the mixture
of respect and surprise in her voice.*

Nora

You don't seem a bit nervous, Miss Delia.

Delia

[Smiling a little.]

Nervous? No; I don't think I am.

3

NORA

I wish I wasn't.
[*As* DELIA *laughs.*]
I wouldn't be so clumsy and slow—
[*She drops a flower.*]
Oh gracious! I keep dropping things.

DELIA

[*Giving her attention to her reflection in
the mirror.*]
You're doing very well, Nora. After all, there's
nothing be be nervous about.

NORA

I know. But you'd think it was *me* getting married
—my hands shake so.

DELIA

Take your time.

NORA

But everybody's gone down.

DELIA

We've still a few moments.

NORA

[*With a little self-conscious laugh.*]
You was always one to take things calm. If it was
me, now—
[*Breaking off to ask anxiously:*]
You're not superstitious either, are you, miss?

DELIA

Not very.

NORA

All the same, you ought to have *"something bor-rowed and something blue—"*

DELIA

[*Taking the words out of her mouth.*]
I know; *"Something old and something new."* My
lace is old; and everything else is new; but I've nothing borrowed or nothing blue.

NORA

I'd feel easier in my mind if you had.

DELIA

[*With an easy, indulgent laugh.*]
Then you'll have to lend me something.

NORA

But what have I got, miss, that you'd wear? It
would have to be something no one would see—

DELIA

A garter! Lend me a garter—

NORA

Oh gracious! Do you mean it, miss?

DELIA

Yes, of course, why not? There's no time to borrow
from anyone else.

NORA

[*Primly.*]
Please look the other way, then.

DELIA

[*Turning her head, again smiling indulgently.*]

I don't see you.

[*As* NORA *turns away and lifts her dress with the greatest possible modesty, a knock at the door causes her to give a little squeal of confusion, drop her skirts quickly, and hurry to open it, as* CHARLOTTE'S *voice calls:*]

CHARLOTTE

[*Through the crack.*]

Delia!

NORA

It's your cousin, miss.

DELIA

Chatty?

CHARLOTTE

[*As* NORA *holds the door open; entering.*]

May I come in?

DELIA

Of course.

[NORA *closes the door.*]

CHARLOTTE

[*Crossing the room, to* DELIA; *importantly.*]

I've something for you.

DELIA

But how pretty you look! I never saw you look so well. Did you, Nora?

NORA

No, miss. I could hardly believe my eyes. It must be the dress.

[CHARLOTTE *laughs shortly; and then speaks simply.*]

CHARLOTTE

Of course it's the dress.

[*She looks down at the dress gratefully.*] I don't often have a dress that's been made especially for me. Thank you for giving me this one.

DELIA

[*Carelessly.*]

Thank mamma. She wanted you to be dressed properly, of course.

NORA

[*Coming forward.*]

Here it is, Miss Delia. Do you want me to put it on, or can you bend down in your new stays?

DELIA

I can bend—

[*She takes the garter, explaining to* CHARLOTTE.]

This is something borrowed.

[CHARLOTTE *politely turns away her head, and* NORA *does the same, as* DELIA *puts on the garter. Then she continues, straightening up:*]

You haven't anything blue I could carry, have you?

CHARLOTTE

[*Drawing a sharp breath.*]

It's odd you should ask me that.

[*Looking at a small box in her hand.*]

This is blue.

DELIA

What is it?

CHARLOTTE

A cameo. It's a present for you—from Clem Spender.

DELIA

[*Abruptly; startled.*]

From Clem! But—

[*To* NORA.]

You may go now, Nora.

NORA

Yes, miss.

[*She slips out with a curious, backward glance, holding up her stocking by clutching at her dress.*]

CHARLOTTE

[*As the door closes on* NORA.]

He asked me to give it to you. He unwrapped it to take out a note that was inside. That's how I saw it was a cameo, and blue. Then he changed his mind again and gave me the note to give you, too.

DELIA

But I thought Clem was in Italy!

CHARLOTTE

[*Simply, but with a hard note in her
voice.*]

He came home today. Just in time for your wedding. He hadn't heard you were going to marry
someone else. He thought you must be ill because
you'd stopped writing.

[*As DELIA opens the note, CHARLOTTE
turns to go, but DELIA stops her before
she can open the door.*]

DELIA

Wait—don't go!

[*CHARLOTTE turns from the door and
stands waiting while DELIA reads the
note. Then CHARLOTTE speaks again,
very simply, but with the same hard note
in her voice, as if she were steeling herself against saying more:*]

CHARLOTTE

They'll play the wedding march next.

DELIA

I know.

[*Suddenly she covers her face with her
hands and speaks impulsively:*]

Oh Chatty, I'm afraid!

CHARLOTTE

Of what?

DELIA

Of Clem! Of what he may say or do. There'll be
champagne, and if he should take a glass too much—.
Watch him, Chatty, will you? Be—be kind to him.

CHARLOTTE

I don't see how anyone could ever be unkind to poor
Clem.

DELIA

[*Bending her head, sharply.*]

Don't—!

CHARLOTTE

[*Coldly, but with some surprise.*]

I didn't know you cared that much.

DELIA

You knew I loved him.

CHARLOTTE

I knew you told him so.

DELIA

I must not cry.

CHARLOTTE

You won't cry if you keep saying to yourself, over
and over: "I'm marrying a Ralston; I'm marrying
a Ralston."

DELIA

[*Defiantly; herself again.*]

Yes, I *am* marrying a Ralston; and I'm glad.

CHARLOTTE

[*Without sympathy.*]

Everyone's glad you're doing so well. They always

expected you to, and you have. But I don't envy you, Delia.

DELIA

I don't want you to envy me; but I don't want you to hold my marriage to Jim against me, either.

CHARLOTTE

[*Stubbornly.*]

When Clem went to Italy to study painting, two years ago, you promised to wait for him.

DELIA

I did wait—but if Clem wanted a wife, he should have stayed here and gone into his uncle's bank, and earned something.

CHARLOTTE

If he'd wanted you for his wife, he should have, of course. Trying to be an artist isn't the sort of thing you had any patience with.

DELIA

But I was patient. He promised to come back, if he failed, and go to work. And if he had, I'd have married him; even though papa disapproved. I swear that.

CHARLOTTE

It never occurred to you, I suppose, that an artist couldn't possibly know whether he was a failure or a success, at the end of a single year?

DELIA

I thought, and I still think, he should have known there was nothing in art, for him, by that time, and

have come back and settled down. And he would
have if he'd cared enough.

CHARLOTTE

He cared. You needn't think he didn't—

DELIA

You needn't think *I* didn't!

CHARLOTTE

[*With feeling.*]

Then why couldn't you have waited?

DELIA

I tell you I did wait! Not one year, but almost two.
It was almost two years after Clem went away before I told Jim I'd marry him instead.

CHARLOTTE

Couldn't you have had the kindness, at least, to write
Clem that you were going to marry someone else?

DELIA

I intended to. I—I—tried to.

CHARLOTTE

But you were ashamed.

DELIA

No, I was not ashamed! I—

[*Wavering a little.*]

I'm fond of Jim. And it seemed hopeless to wait for
Clem.

[*Then frankly, unhappily.*]

I couldn't bear to be an old maid, Chatty.

CHARLOTTE

[*With a strange look of exaltation.*]

I shall be an old maid because the man I love doesn't
love me. Not for any other reason.

CENTER DELIA

[*Frankly surprised; delicately; patroniz-
ingly.*]

Oh, Chatty—my dear! I'm so sorry. I didn't know
there was anyone.

CHARLOTTE

[*Proudly; turning away from* DELIA'S
sudden glance.]

No one has ever known. But I would have waited
for him all my life.

DELIA

You think so, but life doesn't stop; one gets lonely;
one wants children, and a home of one's own.

CHARLOTTE

I could have waited.

[*Then she turns and goes to the door.
There she pauses, listening. Then she
turns back to* DELIA.]

It's the wedding march!

DELIA

[*With an effort.*]

I'm ready.

[*Breathlessly.*]

Remember, watch Clem.

CHARLOTTE

I'll not forget.

DELIA

[*Looking at the cameo.*]

"Something blue."

> [*She slips it into the bosom of her dress, takes her bouquet, and moves across the room towards the door* CHARLOTTE *is holding open. There she pauses long enough to whisper, as she steadies herself by laying a hand on the other's arm:*]

Oh Chatty—I'm trembling!

> [*But almost instantly she recovers her poise, and with her head lifted passes* CHARLOTTE, *disappearing into the passage outside, to the strains of the music, as the curtain falls.*]

SECOND EPISODE
1839

Six years later. The twilight of an autumn day.
CHARLOTTE LOVELL'S *day-nursery in a room*
above the LOVELL *stables in the rear of her grand-*
mother's house in Mercer Street.
An upstairs room. The sloping roof is broken at the
back by a window in an alcove. In the wall at
the left is a narrow door which opens upon a pas-
sage at the head of the stairs. In the wall at the
right a door leads into the coachman's living quar-
ters. A stove stands near the wall above this door.
In the deep alcove at the back are tables of various
heights and sizes, arranged as desks. Behind each
table are chairs or benches; at least ten children
can study here. The room is also furnished with a
round table on which, when the curtain rises, is a
tall lamp, not yet lighted, though the light out-
side the window at the back is already gray; also
several oddly-matched comfortable chairs, a music-
box on another table, a cradle, a small sofa, and,
on the walls, a blackboard and a few prints.
Several poorly dressed children are teasing CLEMEN-
TINA, *a shy little girl, five years old, who faces*

15

them with her back against the side of the biggest arm-chair, one arm reaching back in a clinging gesture for support. Her eyes are miserable and her lips tremble, but she has the air of one who is already used to the taunts of the world.

THE CHILDREN
[*Chanting fiendishly, pointing at* CLEM-ENTINA.]
Tina lives with niggers! Tina lives with niggers!

A BOY
Shame on you, living with niggers!

ANOTHER BOY
Nigger! Nigger!

TINA
I'm not!

A THIRD BOY
You'll turn black yourself some day.

TINA
I will not! I'm white, too.
[*But the others laugh derisively.*]

THE FIRST BOY
You haven't got a poppa or a momma!

TINA
I have.

THE BOY
If you have, they didn't want you. So they gave you to niggers.

THE OTHERS

[*Again in chorus.*]

She lives with niggers! She lives with niggers! She lives with—

> [*The door at the right opens unexpectedly and* CHARLOTTE LOVELL *enters. Although she is angry and upset by what is going on, she seems prettier and happier and even younger in her gray, Quakerish dress than six years ago on the occasion of her cousin* DELIA'S *marriage.*]

CHARLOTTE

[*Instantly.*]

Children! Children!

> [*And instantly they are self-consciously still.* CHARLOTTE *continues severely:*]

How dare you tease Tina! What have I told you? Do you want me to tell your parents you can't come here any more?

> [*The children steal sidelong glances at one another from under their downcast lids. They are now very sober, and a little frightened.*]

CHARLOTTE

Haven't I warned you before?

> [*No one answers.*]

Who began this?

[*Looking from one to the other.*]
Did you, Bennie?

BENNIE

No, ma'am.

CHARLOTTE

Was it you, Emma?

EMMA

No, Miss Lovell. Honest.

CHARLOTTE

Jerry?

[JERRY *shakes his head;* CHARLOTTE *looks
at* TINA:]
Who began it this time, Tina? Don't be afraid to
tell me. Who was it?

TINA

[*Painfully.*]
Nobody.

CHARLOTTE

[*To the others.*]
There! Aren't you ashamed of yourselves?
[*They are, and show it. For an instant*
CHARLOTTE *busies herself picking up
papers and putting the room to rights.
Then she speaks again, but more quietly,
less harshly:*]
In any case, I'm ashamed of you. And if this hap-
pens again, while I'm away, Bridget will speak to
your parents.

[*Recovering her patience.*]
Now put on your things and go home.

> [*The children fetch their coats and caps,
> and put them on in silence.* CHARLOTTE
> *busies herself putting the room to
> rights.*]

EMMA

[*At last; unhappily.*]
I'm sorry, Miss Lovell.

JERRY

[*Also miserable.*]
I didn't mean nothing.

BENNIE

Neither did I.

CHARLOTTE

Very well. But don't let it happen again.
> [*To* EMMA.]

Let me button your coat. It's cold out.

> [*She buttons the child's coat. Suddenly she
> realizes that the other children have their
> heads together, and are trying to make
> up their minds to tell her something.*]

CHARLOTTE

[*Trying to help them.*]
What are you whispering about, children?

TINA

They learned a song to sing for you because you're
going to get married and go away for a while.

CHARLOTTE
[*Pleased.*]
A song? Who taught it to you?

THE CHILDREN
[*All answering at once.*]
Bridget!

CHARLOTTE
Indeed? Well, suppose you let me hear it, then?

THE CHILDREN
[*Singing, self-consciously; after several
false starts.*]

When daylight gets all tired out
I wonder if he looks about
To find some place to go to bed
For room to rest his sleepy head.
For when the stars begin to peep
It's time for me to go to sleep;
And so I take my candle bright
And bid you all a sweet good-night.

[*While they have been singing and "acting
out" the song,* JENNIE MEADE, *a young
woman with a pleasant face and shabby
clothes, has opened the door at the left
and entered quietly; she stands listening,
smiling, then crosses the room to the
cradle.*]
CHARLOTTE
[*To the children.*]

That's very nice. And now good-night and good-bye, until we see each other again.

> [*With another word or two to each, she sends them all away except* TINA, *and they go, reluctantly, with a chorus of good-byes.*]

JENNIE

[*As the door closes on the children.*]

You don't know how much good you've done, Miss Lovell.

> [CHARLOTTE *gives* TINA *a book to look at, as* JENNIE *continues:*]

The way you've helped us poor mothers out by taking care of our children all day, and teaching them nice manners, and to keep clean, and even the ones old enough how to read and write and figure.

CHARLOTTE

But I don't deserve praise for anything I've done, Mrs. Meade. Children interest me.

JENNIE

They wouldn't interest most young ladies in your class—not enough for 'em to give all their time to a lot of strange brats, year after year.

CHARLOTTE

> [*Putting away the papers and books scattered on the desks.*]

But I've had nothing else to do.

JENNIE

You could have been enjoying yourself.

[*Then, with the hesitation of one taking
a liberty.*]

Though I've heard people say you vowed yourself
to God if he'd let you get well of lung-fever that
winter they sent you South.

CHARLOTTE

[*With a smile, as she gives some of the
papers to* JENNIE, *who is nearer the
stove.*]

Oh, that's far from the truth. . . . These can be
burned.

[JENNIE *takes the papers, murmuring
"Yes, ma'am," and puts them in the stove
as* CHARLOTTE *continues, casually:*]

It was something our doctor said one day that gave
me the idea; and as this room over my grandmother's stable wasn't being used, I persuaded her
to let me use it for a nursery where mothers could
leave children who were too young to go to school
and had no one to take care of them while they
were away from home.

[*Then, changing the subject, as if she had
said enough:*]

Your baby is so good.

JENNIE

Yes, the little fellow never cries much. Still, I
couldn't of took him out to work with me. While I
had work.

[CHARLOTTE *notices the despair in her last
words.*]

CHARLOTTE

[*Turns; at blackboard.*]

While you had work. Are you out of work now,
Mrs. Meade?

JENNIE

Yes, ma'am. I lost my place today.

[*Looking down at the child in the cradle,
as she continues to* CHARLOTTE:]

But you've been kindness itself, Miss Lovell, and
now that you're going to get married, I hope you'll
have children of your own to make you happy.

CHARLOTTE

Wait, I've an idea! Bridget, the coachman's wife,
will need someone to help her while I'm on my wed-
ding-trip. Couldn't you come and look after the
children for me?

JENNIE

Oh, I'll be glad to, miss, unless some work should
come my way—

CHARLOTTE

[*Interrupting.*]

I mean to pay you, of course. I can't afford very
much, but I may be able to keep you permanently.
I've really needed another helper for some time.

JENNIE

But you talk like you aim to go on with the nursery,
yourself, after you come back.

CHARLOTTE

I do. I'll be here every day; at least, part of every day.

JENNIE

But won't your husband object—if you don't mind me asking?

CHARLOTTE

I don't expect him to.

JENNIE

But they say he's a very rich man. You'll probably have a big house to look after.

CHARLOTTE

I can look after my nursery, too.

[*She crosses the room, leaving* MRS. MEADE *wondering but at that instant the door at the right is opened by* BRIDGET, *who enters from her kitchen. She is a middle-aged Irishwoman, with a motherly air, and a kind face; and while she wears an apron over her dark neat dress, she hasn't the bearing of the usual servant.*]

BRIDGET

Excuse me, miss—good evening to ye, Mrs. Meade. It's a darling baby ye have to slape so sound and never cry at all.

JENNIE

Good evening, Mrs. O'Connor. Yes, he is good, isn't he?

CHARLOTTE

What is it, Bridget?

BRIDGET

Tina's supper is on the table, miss.

CHARLOTTE

Did you hear, Tina? Aren't you hungry?

TINA

No, ma'am.

CHARLOTTE

Oh, but you must eat, Tina! Go with Bridget—

BRIDGET

Come, Tina—

> [*She holds the door open, and* TINA, *with
> an appealing, timid glance, turns and
> goes obediently into the next room.*
> BRIDGET *follows.* CHARLOTTE *turns back
> to* JENNIE.]

CHARLOTTE

Then we'll consider the matter settled. But I must
tell you that the child who was here just now needs
more attention than the others.

JENNIE

She did look a little peaked, I noticed.

CHARLOTTE

It's not only that; she's had a cold; but the chief
difficulty is that she's very shy and the other children
like to tease her—

> [*Hesitantly.*]

Perhaps I ought to explain that she was left with a

Negro family when a baby, and still lives with them.

JENNIE

The poor little waif! What sort of mother could she have had?

[*Taking up her baby and holding it close as she talks to it:*]

I wouldn't have done that to you, son—even if you'd had no daddy, and the two of us had had nowhere to go but the river.

[*There is a knock on the door at the left, but before* CHARLOTTE *can answer, it is opened by* DR. LANSKELL, *a man well past middle-age, who is obviously very much at home in* CHARLOTTE'S *nursery.*]

CHARLOTTE

[*Pleased at seeing him.*]

Oh, Dr. Lanskell—

DR. LANSKELL

I've brought a very distinguished lady, who's just arrived from Paris, to see you.

CHARLOTTE

[*Eagerly.*]

Not Joe's Aunt Carrie?

DR. LANSKELL

Yes, the dauntless Mrs. Mingott herself, who refuses to be assisted up your narrow stairs.

CHARLOTTE

Oh—let me light the illuminating gas in the passage—

[*She passes him and lights a gas-jet just outside the doorway, calling down to someone on the stairs:*]

Mrs. Mingott!

DR. LANSKELL

[*To* JENNIE, *who has withdrawn to the alcove, her baby in her arms.*]

How's the young man, Mrs. Meade?

JENNIE

[*Smiling, as she looks down at the child.*]

As fine as can be, thank you kindly, Doctor.

[MRS. MINGOTT'S *deep voice sounds from the passage:*]

MRS. MINGOTT

My dear Chatty!

[*Then she enters, preceding* CHARLOTTE *through the narrow doorway.*]

CHARLOTTE

[*Following.*]

How nice of you!

MRS. MINGOTT

[*After one quick, intelligent glance round the room, with the indulgent irony of a worldly-wise person towards a young enthusiast.*]

So this is where you carry on your good works? It seems sanitary. But let me look at you—

[*Her full glance studies* CHARLOTTE.]

I always said you'd never be an old maid, even if you were plain.

CHARLOTTE

[*Meekly, happily.*]

I know you did.

MRS. MINGOTT

Still, you almost fooled me. How old are you now?

CHARLOTTE

Twenty-seven.

DR. LANSKELL

If I hadn't brought her into the world, I wouldn't believe that.

MRS. MINGOTT

I must say she looks six years younger than the last time I saw her, six years ago, at her Cousin Delia's wedding. But love always makes people bloom, no matter what age they are.

CHARLOTTE

[*Noticing* JENNIE, *who edges towards the door as the others move towards the center of the room.*]

Good-night. We'll arrange everything in the morning.

JENNIE

Very well, miss. Good-night.

[*She goes, with a respectful nod to the others, closing the door after her.*]

MRS. MINGOTT

One of your paupers, I suppose?

[*Without waiting for an answer, to* CHAR-
LOTTE:]

My nephew's—twenty-nine. So it was high time he
was getting married, too. I should say it was now
or never for both of you.

CHARLOTTE

That's what we thought, too, Mrs. Mingott.

MRS. MINGOTT

You must call me "Aunt Carrie" now.

CHARLOTTE

[*Shyly.*]

Thank you.

MRS. MINGOTT

Yes, you're both getting on. And everyone had decided you'd both settled down to single blessedness
for life. How did you ever happen to take a fancy to
each other after all these years?

CHARLOTTE

I suppose it was because we've seen each other so
often since my cousin married Joe's brother.

MRS. MINGOTT

But Joe wrote me you put him off nearly a year after
he proposed. Why didn't you jump at such a chance?
You must have known you weren't likely to have
another like it.

CHARLOTTE

I—I—

MRS. MINGOTT

However, it's none of my business, and you may tell
me so, if you like.

CHARLOTTE

I'm not going to do that. But do sit down—
          [*To* DR. LANSKELL.]
Won't you, too?

DR. LANSKELL

Not until I've looked at little Tina—

MRS. MINGOTT

          [*From the chair* CHARLOTTE *has just
          placed for her.*]
He's had his orders. I want to talk to *you.*

CHARLOTTE

          [*Just a little nervously, from behind the
          chair.*]
How nice!

          [*To* DR. LANSKELL, *as she opens the door
          to the kitchen, and he goes in:*]
You'll find Tina with Bridget. I think she's over her
cold; but I'm glad you're going to see her.

DR. LANSKELL

We'll make sure.

          [*Then he goes, and she closes the door
          after him.*]

CHARLOTTE

          [*Turning to* MRS. MINGOTT.]
Are you warm? It's very cold out.

          [*She goes towards the stove.*]

Mrs. Mingott

I'm never cold. Come here; don't fuss . . . I want to say something and get it over with, before anyone interrupts us.

> [Charlotte *comes and stands near her uncertainly.*]

Sit down here beside me.

> [Charlotte *obeys, sitting on a child's chair at* Mrs. Mingott's *side.*]

Don't look so frightened. I only want to find out what you want for a wedding present.

Charlotte

Mrs. Mingott—!

Mrs. Mingott

My dear girl, I know you've always gone to parties in made-over dresses, and I know there must be things you'd like, but which you've too much pride to ask for. There are—aren't there?

Charlotte

> [*Simply.*]

Of course.

Mrs. Mingott

Then tell me, what do you need most?

> [Charlotte *looks up wistfully, but doesn't answer.*]

Out with it. What is it—?

Charlotte

I—I'm not sure. I don't really know.

MRS. MINGOTT

[*Bluntly.*]

Then in that case you mustn't be offended if I give you money.

CHARLOTTE

[*Startled.*]

Money!

[*She bites her lip, and then speaks quickly, humbly, in a voice charged with emotion:*]

Oh, dear Mrs. Mingott, how did you happen to think I'd need—I'd want—some money of my own—?

MRS. MINGOTT

Because I know your relatives, my child, as well as my own; and I know there's not one of them, including Joe, who realizes how much a modest little sum— shall we say five hundred dollars—?

CHARLOTTE

[*Radiantly.*]

Oh!

MRS. MINGOTT

—means to any girl, even when she's marrying a rich man.

CHARLOTTE

You're too good. But—

[*Hopelessly.*]

But—I—I'd like you to know—I want to tell you—

MRS. MINGOTT

[*As* CHARLOTTE *pauses, unable to go on.*]
Well? What are you trying to say? Don't stammer
and blush. *Say it.*

CHARLOTTE

I—I'd like to tell you what I'd use it for, and then,
of course, if—if you don't want me to, you must
say so.

MRS. MINGOTT

We won't talk about that. I'm giving you the money
to do with as you like.

CHARLOTTE

[*Haltingly, after a little pause.*]
I was ill—you know—

MRS. MINGOTT

Yes, yes, child; we all expected you to go like your
poor father.

CHARLOTTE

But I didn't go like my father . . . I didn't die . . . I
got well. But when I came home I—I was lonely. I
couldn't do the things I'd done before. That's why—
for four years now—I've taken care of these poor
children. And you can't know—no one can know—
what they've come to mean to me—how much I love
them—how much they need me—

MRS. MINGOTT

[*A little stiffly, as* CHARLOTTE *pauses, carried away by her own emotion.*]
No doubt your efforts are meritorious.

CHARLOTTE

And now that I'm going to be married, grand-mamma can't understand why I don't want to give them up.

MRS. MINGOTT

[*Drily.*]

Probably she thinks you'll have children of your own.

CHARLOTTE

[*Hurriedly.*]

Yes—but—one can't give up a thing one's been doing, that it's one's duty to keep on doing, because of something that may happen—that I hope will happen—but that hasn't happened yet.

MRS. MINGOTT

Does my nephew know your attitude on this subject?

CHARLOTTE

He knows how I feel about them; but, of course, I can't expect him to feel as I do. So having some money of my own—five hundred dollars—will make everything different, you see.

MRS. MINGOTT

No; I don't see. How will it make *anything* different?

CHARLOTTE

I won't have to begin by asking him to help me, if grandmamma should refuse to let me go on with my nursery here. With five hundred dollars, I can manage everything—another room somewhere, and a

woman to help take care of the children—for some
time, at least.

> [*A bare pause;* MRS. MINGOTT *looks at*
> CHARLOTTE, *but for once finds nothing
> to say. Then* CHARLOTTE *adds tensely:*]

So, thanks—thanks—a thousand times.

> [*And abruptly kisses* MRS. MINGOTT'S
> *hand.*]

MRS. MINGOTT
> [*Drawing it away.*]

Tut, tut . . .

> [*There is a knock on the door, and* DELIA,
> *luxurious in her furs and velvet, enters,
> followed by two tall young men who look
> very much alike, and are distinguished
> by the same mannerisms; they are* JAMES
> *and* JOSEPH RALSTON.]

CHARLOTTE
> [*Rising; very much surprised.*]

Delia—and—

DELIA
> [*Gaily, as she enters.*]

Mr. James Ralston; and Mr. Joseph Ralston who is
very much afraid that he'll be sent away because it's
half an hour before he was told to call. Aunt Carrie . . .

> [*As* DELIA *kisses* MRS. MINGOTT, CHAR-
> LOTTE *gives one hand to* JAMES *and the
> other to* JOSEPH.]

JOSEPH

Send me away if you don't want me, but Delia and
Jim were stopping for Aunt Carrie—

CHARLOTTE

[*As* JOSEPH *lifts the hand she has given
him to his lips.*]

Of course I'll not send you away.

[*Then rather pointedly.*]

And I'm glad Delia and Jim found a reason for
visiting my nursery at last. They've never been here
before.

DELIA

[*Smoothly.*]

But that doesn't mean we haven't been interested.

CHARLOTTE

[*With a trace of resentment.*]

I'm afraid it does.

MRS. MINGOTT

Tut, tut, don't bicker, children. Naturally, no one's
interested in Chatty's waifs except herself. But now
that we're here we might as well look them over.

JOSEPH

[*To* CHARLOTTE, *without enthusiasm, but
not without sympathy.*]

But they must have gone by this time. Haven't they?

CHARLOTTE

[*Uncertainly.*]

All but one, who always has her supper here, with
Bridget, because she's more delicate than the others—

JAMES

[*Interrupting explosively.*]

Delicate!

CHARLOTTE

[*With a laugh.*]

Don't be alarmed.

JAMES

But if she's not in good health—

MRS. MINGOTT

[*Sensibly.*]

I'm sure there's no danger, Jim. Lanskell's here now, and if there were, he wouldn't let it be brought in. Let us see the child, Chatty!

CHARLOTTE

[*Hesitantly, to* JOSEPH.]

Shall I?

JOSEPH

I don't see why not.

CHARLOTTE

[*After another instant's hesitation, impulsively.*]

Then I will!

[*She disappears, hurrying through the door at the right, closing it after her.*]

JAMES

[*Gloomily, in a voice full of doubt.*]

I hope it *is* in good health.

DELIA

Jim, my dear, we *must* be nice about this. We simply must.

JAMES

Be as nice as you please, but don't let it come too close, my dear. Keep it at a distance.

[DELIA *laughs; he continues a little heatedly:*]

Remember, there's an epidemic of diphtheria about; and we've got our own child to think of.

MRS. MINGOTT

You sound just like your father, Jim; and your grandfather.

JAMES

[*Frowning; determined not to be smiled out of his uneasiness.*]

You heard Chatty say it was delicate. And "delicate" might mean anything.

MRS. MINGOTT

Pooh!

DELIA

[*Tactfully.*]

Of course, there's no real danger; but ever since the Van de Luyden's little boy caught smallpox at the circus, last year, Jim's been in terror for fear something of the sort might happen to little Dee.

JOSEPH

[*Abruptly, with a gust of feeling.*]

If Jim's afraid of your simply looking at one of these

children, whom Chatty's with every day, how do you
suppose I feel about *her?* When she's not strong?

DELIA

[*Quietly.*]
Chatty's perfectly well now, Joe.

JOSEPH

She went away once—to die. I can't forget that.

> [*He turns his back on them all, and goes
> and looks out the window.*]

DELIA

[*Again changing the subject tactfully.*]
What did you do today, Aunt Carrie?

MRS. MINGOTT

What one usually does after being abroad six years.
I went to my bank, I saw my lawyer, and my dentist.

JAMES

[*Sympathetically.*]
I hope you found your affairs in good order.

MRS. MINGOTT

My affairs are always in good order.

JAMES

And I hope you haven't been suffering from toothache.

MRS. MINGOTT

I never suffer from toothache!

DELIA

It doesn't sound like a very pleasant day.

MRS. MINGOTT

It was. They were all pleased as Punch to see me,

and I was pleased to see them. Of course, when I was young, things were different. One didn't exchange personalities on such occasions. I remember my mother taught me never to recognize even my most intimate friends while shopping—she felt it so unbecoming to mix business with pleasure.

> [DELIA *and* JAMES *are amused; even* JOSEPH *turns from the window, smiling, and saunters towards them.*]

DELIA
[*Out of the pause which has followed.*]
Aunt Carrie doesn't look a day older than when she came back for our wedding, does she, Jim?

JAMES
[*Gallantly.*]
Not an hour.

MRS. MINGOTT
[*Showing herself impervious to flattery.*]
Nonsense; but whether I've changed or not, this city has. I don't know where I am when I look about.

JOSEPH
Yes, all sorts of changes began, after the big fire in '35 destroyed so many old landmarks.

MRS. MINGOTT
I've never heard yet what caused it.

JAMES
[*With feeling.*]

These modern abominations; gas pipes, and high
buildings of four and even five stories.

MRS. MINGOTT

And two years later your banks stopped payments.
That was a pretty to-do. That and your riots. I hear
there were mobs in front of the City Hall demanding
bread.

JAMES

[*Unsympathetically.*]

They should have been shot down like mad dogs. Instead, they broke into a warehouse and threw five
hundred barrels of flour into the street.

DELIA

They say it looked as if it had been snowing.

MRS. MINGOTT

Do you wonder I prefer Paris? At least they've had
their revolution there.

[*The door at the right is opened and* DR.
LANSKELL *enters.*]

MRS. MINGOTT

[*Instantly; without waiting for him to exchange greetings with the others.*]

I suppose Chatty's taking all this time to make the
child presentable.

DR. LANSKELL

She wanted her to finish her supper.

JAMES

Tell me, Doctor, do you consider these children perfectly healthy?

DR. LANSKELL

As sound as pumpkins, all of them; thanks to Chatty.

> [*The door is opened again, and* CHAR-
> LOTTE *returns, leading* CLEMENTINA *by
> the hand.*]

CHARLOTTE

> [*Proudly.*]

This is Tina.

> [*The child stands still, averting her eyes.*]

JOSEPH

> [*Gently.*]

Good evening, Tina.

> [TINA *lifts her eyes to him, then drops
> them quickly.*]

CHARLOTTE

> [*Anxiously.*]

Don't be so shy, darling.

> [*She leads her forward.*]

This is Mrs. Mingott, Tina... Now what do you do?

> [TINA *makes a faltering, delicate curtsy.*]

CHARLOTTE

That's right.

MRS. MINGOTT

> [*In her bold voice, staring at the child.*]

Tina what?

> [*As* TINA *doesn't answer; impatiently:*]

What is your other name, child?

TINA

[*In a shy little voice.*]
Clementina.

MRS. MINGOTT

But your other name?

[*The child looks up at* CHARLOTTE, *help-lessly.*]

CHARLOTTE

[*Quietly.*]
She doesn't understand.

MRS. MINGOTT

How old are you, Clementina?

[*The child looks at* CHARLOTTE *again.*]

CHARLOTTE

[*Prompting her.*]
Five.

TINA

Five.

MRS. MINGOTT

But don't you know your parents' name, Clementina?

CHARLOTTE

[*Sharply.*]
No. She doesn't.

MRS. MINGOTT

[*Ominously.*]
Oh... !

[*The child coughs suddenly.*]

JAMES

There!

DR. LANSKELL

That's nothing.

[TINA *coughs again.*]

JAMES

She looks as if she might have a fever—

CHARLOTTE

[*Quickly.*]

But she hasn't—has she, Dr. Lanskell?

DR. LANSKELL

No, she's only coughing to tease us; aren't you, Tina?

[TINA *smiles at him shyly.*]

MRS. MINGOTT

Can't a child sneeze twice?

CHARLOTTE

She always has a high colour.

[CHARLOTTE *passes her hand nervously over the child's brow.*]

MRS. MINGOTT

Let's hear her talk. Where did you get your pretty name, little girl?

[TINA *looks wistfully to* CHARLOTTE.]

CHARLOTTE

She doesn't know.

MRS. MINGOTT

[*Again to* TINA.]

Where do you live?

[*Again the child seems unable to answer,
and looks imploringly to* CHARLOTTE.]

CHARLOTTE

She—she's a very sensitive child. . . . We never talk
to her about such things.

MRS. MINGOTT

About where she lives? Doesn't she *know* where she
lives?

DR. LANSKELL

Oh yes, she knows.

CHARLOTTE

[*Protectively.*]

Come here, Tina.

[*She draws the child away, towards the
stove at one side of the room, in order to
keep her from hearing, and tries to di-
vert her attention by putting a book in
her hands.*]

DR. LANSKELL

[*Continuing in a guarded voice.*]

And she knows enough already, I think, to be
ashamed of living with Negroes.

MRS. MINGOTT

All the same, children should learn to speak when
they're spoken to—

[*Then breaking off abruptly, and echoing:*]

Negroes! She isn't the hundred-dollar baby?

[*The others are suddenly deeply interested.*
CHARLOTTE *whispers to the child to pre-*
vent her listening.]

MRS. MINGOTT
[*To* DR. LANSKELL.]
Is she?

DR. LANSKELL
[*Vaguely.*]
You mean—?

MRS. MINGOTT
[*Sharply.*]
I mean the baby who, according to gossip, was left
several years ago on the threshold of one of those
disgraceful shanties out on Broadway near Nine-
teenth Street, with a hundred dollar bill pinned to its
bib. You must remember all the talk it caused. Everyone wrote me—

DELIA
[*Calling, rather breathlessly, as* MRS. MIN-
GOTT *pauses abruptly, speculation in her*
eyes.]
Chatty—

[CHARLOTTE, *leaving* TINA, *turns and*
comes forward.]

CHARLOTTE
Yes?

DELIA
Is this the hundred-dollar baby, Chatty?

CHARLOTTE

[*To* DR. LANSKELL, *casually.*]

Is she?

DR. LANSKELL

[*As if recalling an unimportant fact.*]

Yes, yes, of course. I'd almost forgotten how Jessamine and Cyrus came by the child.

[*Smiling.*]

At least, I'd forgotten that sensational hundred dollar bill.

DELIA

[*Almost accusingly, to* CHARLOTTE.]

Didn't you know that, Chatty, really?

CHARLOTTE

[*Simply.*]

I knew only that she was a foundling whom a Negro family had taken in.

DELIA

And you didn't know that she was *the* hundred-dollar baby?

CHARLOTTE

I'd never thought of it.

JOSEPH

Naturally she never thought of it. I'd rather we changed the subject.

MRS. MINGOTT

[*Tartly.*]

The subject would never have been mentioned if

Chatty herself hadn't given us to understand the child was illegitimate.

JOSEPH

She did nothing of the sort. She never used such a word in her life. All she said was that the child didn't know who her parents were—

MRS. MINGOTT

She said "a foundling"—

JOSEPH

She thought—

CHARLOTTE

[*Quietly.*]

I knew what the word meant, Joe.

JOSEPH

[*Giving in a little but still indignant.*]

But that's not the same thing as going back and delving into a scandal that would disgust—that *has* disgusted her. I'd rather we didn't say any more about it.

MRS. MINGOTT

I'm sorry, my dear boy, that I offended you by a little plain speaking in Charlotte's presence. But, after all, her work must have taught her some of the unpleasant facts of life. *I* never knew when *I* was a girl that people who weren't married *could* have babies.

[*Then with her usual abruptness, looking round, calling loudly:*]

Come here, Clementina.

[*The child turns and comes forward,
slowly.* MRS. MINGOTT *repeats:*]
Come here, and let me look at you.

[*The child comes and stops a little distance
away from her, in the shelter of* CHAR-
LOTTE'S *presence.*]

MRS. MINGOTT

[*Staring at her; confidentially to* CHAR-
LOTTE.]
She has blood. Look at her feet—

CHARLOTTE

You'll make her afraid; she's very timid—

MRS. MINGOTT

She walks as if her ancestors knew how to dance.

[*Then to the child:*]
Do you like to dance, Clementina?

[TINA *does not answer at once, but looks
round vaguely.*]

CHARLOTTE

You like to dance, don't you, Tina? Shall we play
the music-box?

[*But before she can answer,* MRS. MIN-
GOTT *speaks again.*]

MRS. MINGOTT

Haven't you been taught to speak when you're
spoken to, little girl? What's the matter? Has the
cat got your tongue?

CHARLOTTE

[*Crossing to the door at the right, and calling into the kitchen.*]

Bridget, come and take Tina now.

[*But almost at the same instant,* DELIA *calls to* TINA, *softly, pityingly:*]

DELIA

Tina—

[*The child turns and looks at her for the first time.* DELIA *leans forward and holds out her hand.* TINA, *after one hesitating glance, runs toward her.* MRS. MINGOTT *is not pleased.* CHARLOTTE *is astonished.*]

MRS. MINGOTT

Come back here, Tina—

[*Bridget enters and pauses near the kitchen door, waiting.*]

DELIA

Please, Aunt Carrie—

[*She takes the child upon her lap.*]

JAMES

[*Anxiously.*]

She coughed, remember—

[*But* DELIA *and* TINA *are making friends. They have eyes only for one another.* JAMES *turns to the doctor again.*]

You say there's nothing to fear?

DR. LANSKELL
Nothing.

BRIDGET
Mind her feet, ma'am. Mind your feet, Tina; don't let them soil the lady's pretty dress.

[*Then to* CHARLOTTE.]

Her shoes ain't none too clean, as we know, miss.

[*But* CHARLOTTE *does not hear. She is absorbed in watching* TINA *and* DELIA, *although the child is doing no more than looking up at* DELIA, *and* DELIA *does no more than smile at* TINA.]

MRS. MINGOTT
[*Drily.*]

Evidently she's not afraid of Delia.

JAMES
[*Proudly; inconsistently well pleased.*]

Children always take to her like that.

DELIA
[*Turning suddenly towards* BRIDGET.]

Do you need any new toys?

BRIDGET
[*Impulsively.*]

That we do, ma'am, though Miss Charlotte will tell you different—being as she doesn't like to beg from her friends for our poor darlin's.

[*To* CHARLOTTE.]

Begging your pardon, miss.

DELIA

[*Happily, her smile still on* TINA.]

You may beg from me. I wish you would . . . I'll
send you some, tomorrow. And some clothes my little girl has outgrown, if you think you can use them,
too.

> [BRIDGET *turns to* CHARLOTTE *as if ex-
> pecting her to answer, but* CHARLOTTE
> *looks as if she has not heard.*]

BRIDGET

[*A little more heartily than is necessary.*]

Indade we can, ma'am. And the toys will come in
very handy while Miss Charlotte's away on her
honeymoon—for the little things will be lonesome
without her.

JAMES

[*To* DELIA.]

It's nearly five, my dear, and we haven't seen your
grandmother yet. If we're to be home in time to
hear little Dee say Grace before her supper—

DELIA

[*Interrupting, obediently.*]

I know. . . . Shall we go?

> [*She stirs, as if to put down the child, who
> suddenly clings to her.* DELIA *laughs
> with pleased surprise.*]

Why, Tina—!

BRIDGET

[*Even more surprised.*]

She doesn't want to leave go of you, ma'am. Come,
Teeny—

[*Then to* CHARLOTTE.]

I never saw her take to anybody like that before,
miss.

CHARLOTTE

[*Speaking at last; sternly; almost harshly.*]

Come, Tina.

DELIA

[*As the child takes her arms from her
neck; holding her close, impetuously.*]

Do you want this lovely yellow chain, Tina?

TINA

Oh!

[DELIA *puts the chain around* TINA'S
neck.]

BRIDGET

[*Almost exploding.*]

Good gracious, ma'am—you can't leave that fine
chain on her when she has to go back to those
blacks!

JAMES

Of course you can't.

CHARLOTTE

[*In a voice not to be disobeyed.*]

Come, Tina. Bridget is waiting.

[*She takes the chain from the child's neck
and hands it to* DELIA, *speaking briefly:*]

Here's your chain.

DELIA

[*Who has risen as soon as* TINA *has slid from her lap, warmly, bending over* TINA.]

But I'll come again soon; and let her wear it again. Good-bye, Clementina.

[*She bends and kisses the child, who again winds her arms about her neck.*]

TINA

Goo'-bye.

[*Then she turns and takes the hand* BRIDGET *is holding out, as* DELIA *laughs.*]

CHARLOTTE

[*Sharply.*]

Tell the others good-bye, too, Tina.

TINA

[*Turning and speaking indifferently.*]

Goo'-bye.

JOSEPH, JAMES *and* DR. LANSKELL

[*At the same time.*]

Good-bye, Tina ... Good-bye, Clementina.

[*Then* BRIDGET *and the child disappear through the doorway at the right.*]

DELIA

[*As if nothing unusual has happened.*]

The darling!

[*To* MRS. MINGOTT.]

Will you come with us, Aunt Carrie?

MRS. MINGOTT

[*Rising.*]

Yes.

[*The word has a slightly grim, displeased sound. But* DELIA *does not notice.* JAMES *goes to the door at the left and holds it open.* MRS. MINGOTT, *not choosing to speak again, passes him and disappears into the passage beyond.* JAMES *waits for* DELIA. DR. LANSKELL *follows.*]

DELIA

Why can't we take you home for dinner with us, Dr. Lanskell?

JAMES

[*Heartily, as they go out into the passage.*]

Yes, why not? Come along and take pot-luck.

[DR. LANSKELL'S *answer is heard indistinctly.*]

DELIA

[*Calling back.*]

Coming, Chatty?

JOSEPH

[*Answering for her.*]

In a moment.

[*He closes the door and turns to* CHARLOTTE. *For an instant their eyes meet; then he catches her hand, and slowly draws her into his arms.*]

My darling. . . .

[*He kisses her tenderly and holds her close.
For an instant her face rests against his
shoulder, then suddenly she puts her
lips to his with a passionate impulse;
JOSEPH'S kiss answers it, then just as
suddenly, he draws back in confusion.*]

CHARLOTTE
[*In a low voice, a little hard, as she moves
out of his arms.*]
I've shocked you.

JOSEPH
[*Self-consciously, holding her by the
wrists.*]
How?

CHARLOTTE
[*In the same low, hard voice.*]
You know.

JOSEPH
I don't understand. . . .

CHARLOTTE
Yes, you do.

JOSEPH
[*Trying to draw her back into his em-
brace, reassurance in his voice.*]
But after all, we're almost married—

CHARLOTTE
Only we're not. And I should keep my kisses for my
husband. Nice girls do.

JOSEPH

[*With his arms about her again.*]

I understand you, Chatty. . . . You feel things more
than other people.

CHARLOTTE

[*Gratefully.*]

Yes, I think I must.

JOSEPH

And you show what you feel.

CHARLOTTE

[*Timidly.*]

Too much—?

JOSEPH

Not with me; *not* when we're *alone.* But sometimes
there's something in your face and voice that I'd
rather not share with other people.

CHARLOTTE

I don't understand you. When?

JOSEPH

When you're with these waifs, for instance.

CHARLOTTE

Oh!

JOSEPH

Even when you're talking about them, people catch
glimpses of how much you'll love *our* children when
they come.

[*She moves away; he follows her, continuing quickly:*]

Forgive me, dearest, if it seems lacking in delicacy

to talk of that now, but if I could keep all of you
for myself—and them—I would. You see, I'm
jealous.

CHARLOTTE

[*With a little laugh; half pleased, half
disturbed.*]

Jealous! Of my waifs? Oh, Joe!

JOSEPH

[*Smiling.*]

I know it's foolish, but I admit it. Even if you can't
understand it.

CHARLOTTE

[*Abruptly; wryly; but feeling very sure
of him.*]

One thing no one can understand is your marrying
me. . . . Even grandmamma—who's fond of me—
can't understand it. There are so many younger girls
—most of them prettier—and all better off!

JOSEPH

Chatty!

CHARLOTTE

[*Slyly.*]

And too innocent to have ever even heard of the
hundred-dollar baby!

JOSEPH

[*Gravely.*]

My dear, you must forgive Aunt Carrie for speaking so freely; it's living in Paris so long.

CHARLOTTE

[*Interrupting; still teasing him a little, and wincing at the same time.*]

—and of course Delia never thought that I'd do as well as she did! I'm sure she thinks I'm cheating you, Joe—

JOSEPH

[*As she interrupts herself with a short laugh; impatiently; not amused, and not wanting* CHARLOTTE *to indulge in such thoughts.*]

Of course she doesn't, but if she did—would it matter? Do we have to care what Delia or anybody else thinks?

CHARLOTTE

[*Soberly; with a note of elation.*]

No! And that's what's so wonderful—that I don't have to care what anybody thinks any longer. They've all stopped patronizing me now—now that I'm not going to be a poor relation all my life—an old maid—to fetch and carry for everyone!

[*Then in a different voice, self-controlled again.*]

Your aunt was ever so kind. Do you know what she's giving me for a wedding present?

JOSEPH

What?

CHARLOTTE

Five hundred dollars to do exactly as I like with—

JOSEPH

But you don't need money—

CHARLOTTE

And do you know what I'm going to do with it?

JOSEPH

Aunt Carrie means well, but—

CHARLOTTE

I've told her; I'm going to use it for my nursery.
You don't mind?

JOSEPH

[*Frowning.*]

I'd prefer to give you what you want for your
paupers, myself.

CHARLOTTE

[*Softly.*]

You can still give me what I want most for them.

JOSEPH

[*Cautiously.*]

What is that?

CHARLOTTE

Your interest, your advice, your presence.

JOSEPH

[*Blankly.*]

My presence? Where?

CHARLOTTE

Here. With me. A little while, every day—or at least
as often as it's convenient for you to come in. I
want you to learn to know them as I know them;
and pity them—and feel towards them as I do.

JOSEPH

You're really counting on still coming here every day?

CHARLOTTE

Certainly; it never occured to me that I wouldn't!

JOSEPH

It never occurred to me that you would.

CHARLOTTE

But why shouldn't I?

JOSEPH

Why should you?

CHARLOTTE

You *know!* Because of all these unfortunate children mean to me; and all I mean to them. Because it's my duty.

JOSEPH

Duty! A married woman's first duty is to her husband, her home—

CHARLOTTE

Joe! You're not really expecting me to desert them? You couldn't—!

JOSEPH

[*Stubbornly.*]

You'll have other things to do. Your life will be different. You should have realized that, yourself.

CHARLOTTE

[*After an instant; profoundly miserable.*]

But—I owe it to them. I—I've promised their poor parents to go on helping them.

JOSEPH

[*Gently, trying to smile.*]

Don't you think you owe me and yourself more than
you owe these strangers, Chatty? After all, you've
done more than your share for them during the past
four years.

CHARLOTTE

You've said yourself it was one of the reasons you
cared for me—that you felt I'd tried to do something
for others.

JOSEPH

[*Not yielding.*]

It's true. No one has admired your unselfishness
more than I have.

CHARLOTTE

But it wasn't unselfishness, Joe. I liked what I was
doing; and now that I'm going to be married and
feel myself so lucky—I want more than ever to go
on helping those less fortunate than myself. You
don't really want me to give them up, do you, just
because you're giving me so much?

JOSEPH

[*Uncomfortable; touched.*]

Not—not altogether, perhaps.

CHARLOTTE

What does that mean?

JOSEPH

I want you to indulge in any charitable work that
interests you. But in a proper manner.

CHARLOTTE

A proper manner. Giving money—you mean?

JOSEPH

Naturally; now that you'll have money to give.

CHARLOTTE

Oh, Joe, as if that were enough—!

JOSEPH

[*Rigidly.*]

Money's not to be despised.

CHARLOTTE

Of course it isn't. Only—

JOSEPH

[*Pompously, as she halts, unable to go on.*]

And I've no objections if you wish to visit them, now and then.

CHARLOTTE

Visit them!

JOSEPH

You can easily find some suitable person whom I'll pay to take care of them.

CHARLOTTE

But I'm to give up looking after them, myself?

JOSEPH

Certainly. I couldn't permit you to come here every day yourself.

CHARLOTTE

Oh!

[*She covers her face with her hands.*]

JOSEPH

[*Miserably; feeling he understands her in-
tensity, although she is in the wrong.*]

Don't—don't take it like that, my darling.

CHARLOTTE

But why can't I look after them myself? Why can't
I come here every day and see them? If only for a
little while?

JOSEPH

You'll have other things to do; and certain responsibilities. Things will be different after we're married.
And much pleasanter for you, I hope.

[*As she doesn't answer, but averts her
face, stubbornly, he continues, as pa-
tiently as possible.*]

You'll have a house of your own to see to, and in
time, children of your own.

CHARLOTTE

But, until then—?

JOSEPH

[*Sharply.*]

Don't you see people would think it odd?

CHARLOTTE

[*Understanding.*]

Oh, *people!*

JOSEPH

[*Arguing against her stubborn looks.*]

Before, when you'd nothing else to do, they could
understand. But now—

CHARLOTTE

[*Interrupting.*]

Because I'm making a good marriage, I'm supposed to get rid of these poor darlings as if they were dolls I'd finished playing with. Oh, no! I can't! I won't!

JOSEPH

[*Frightened.*]

You refuse—?

CHARLOTTE

[*Also frightened, brokenly.*]

They need me.

JOSEPH

I need you—

CHARLOTTE

It's not the same thing. I'd be giving them only a little part of each day. Why can't I do that?

JOSEPH

I've explained.

CHARLOTTE

[*Ironically.*]

You've explained that people might think it odd.

JOSEPH

[*Doggedly.*]

Then there's the actual danger—

CHARLOTTE

Danger?

JOSEPH

Of disease.

CHARLOTTE

That's absurd!

JOSEPH

All sorts of diseases can be carried. And you're not strong.

CHARLOTTE

I'm not afraid.

JOSEPH

Jim was afraid for Delia even to look at little Tina.

CHARLOTTE

Oh, Jim! Delia! As if they made any difference!

JOSEPH

It shows that I'm not unreasonable in thinking of your health.

CHARLOTTE

[*Desperately.*]

It shows you're a Ralston, Joe! And afraid of anything that everybody else doesn't do. And afraid of the slightest risk to your own comfort and safety!

[*Then as he picks up his hat to go, she puts out her hand, and adds miserably.*]

We're quarrelling, Joe.

JOSEPH

I can't help being what I am. But I loved you and I thought you loved me.

CHARLOTTE

I do! Oh, I do! You know I do...

JOSEPH

[*Reluctantly; touched.*]

I don't want to quarrel. If we quarrelled now, we might never make it up.

CHARLOTTE

I know that . . . I'm thinking of that. I'm thinking of everything!

[*She covers her face with her hands.*]

JOSEPH

I am right; and you are wrong. But we'd better not talk about it any more until we're both more collected

CHARLOTTE

[*After an instant, passionately.*]

It's not fair of you to ask me to give up these children!

JOSEPH

[*Doggedly.*]

Very well, it's not fair; but I ask it all the same.

CHARLOTTE

[*Decisively.*]

Then—

[*But she doesn't finish.*]

JOSEPH

After all, they're only a dozen or so strange waifs—

CHARLOTTE

[*Impatiently, miserably.*]

No. Let's not talk any more. Not now—

JOSEPH

I won't. I'm going.

CHARLOTTE

[*Dully.*]

Good-bye.

JOSEPH

Don't say that—yet. After all, what I'm asking isn't much. You—you'll see that . . . I'll be waiting for you to send for me—when you do see it.

[*She stares at him hopelessly; he at her, hopefully; then he turns and goes. As the door at the left closes behind him,* BRIDGET *opens the door at the right, and enters with* TINA. *Both wear their wraps.*]

BRIDGET

I'm taking Teeny home meself, miss. Though I'll lose me man if he has to wait for his supper many more times.

CHARLOTTE

He won't have to wait after this. Mrs. Meade is coming to help us. You might stop and ask her to begin tomorrow.

BRIDGET

[*In some surprise.*]

But the children ain't to come tomorrow, miss. Being as it's Saturday and you jump the broomstick Tuesday.

CHARLOTTE

Of course. I remember, now. Come here, Tina.

[*The child runs to her;* CHARLOTTE *drops*

*on her knees beside her, putting her arms
about her, and holding her close, as she
speaks yearningly.*]

Kiss me good-night, darling.

[*The child lifts her face and lets CHAR-
LOTTE kiss her. A servant with a shawl
about her shoulders opens the door at
the left and looks in.*]

SERVANT

The dressmakers are asking for you, miss.

[*As CHARLOTTE turns, TINA, released
from her embrace, wanders away, and
goes to the music-box.*]

SERVANT

[*Continuing, as CHARLOTTE does not
answer or move.*]

They've brought the wedding dress for your last
fitting.

[TINA *makes the music-box play and begins dancing to its gay tune. The
servant continues, as CHARLOTTE does
not answer.*]

Shall I say you're coming soon, miss?

CHARLOTTE

[*In a flat voice.*]

I suppose so.

SERVANT

Yes, miss.

[*She goes, closing the door.*]

CHARLOTTE

[*Looking at* TINA, *who continues to dance in the gathering shadows of the room.*]

Come, Tina; kiss me good-night again, child—

[TINA *comes, reluctantly, and lifts her face, and* CHARLOTTE *draws her into her arms, as the curtain falls.*]

THIRD EPISODE
1839

Several hours later.

The lamps and candles are lighted in the JAMES
RALSTONS' *front drawing-room in Gramercy
Square and a fire burns in the fireplace in the wall
between this room and the next. Above the fireplace is a doorway. Opposite in the wall at the
right are two tall, deeply curtained windows. In
the wall at the back is the doorway opening upon
the entrance passage.*

MRS. MINGOTT *and* DELIA, *informally dressed for
the evening, are passing the time until the gentlemen come from the dining-room in casual conversation. Delia, in the light from one lamp, bends
over her embroidery; and* MRS. MINGOTT, *in the
light from another, looks at photographs in an
album through a pearl-handled magnifying glass.*

DELIA

[*Out of a pause.*]

You're not tired?

MRS. MINGOTT

I'm never tired.

[*After another pause.*]

71

You're a very good housekeeper, my dear. That was an excellent dinner.

DELIA

It was very simple.

MRS. MINGOTT

One doesn't want any other kind when one's just off a boat.

DELIA

I hope you didn't feel the motion too much.

MRS. MINGOTT

I never feel the motion. How did you ever persuade Jim to let you dine at six instead of two?

DELIA

[Looking up, inwardly amused.]

It wasn't easy.

MRS. MINGOTT

You don't need to tell me that. I know my Ralston relatives.

DELIA

But I managed it. Though you should have seen Jim's face the first time I proposed it.

[She smiles as she remembers.]

He looked exactly like that funny portrait of the first Ralston.

MRS. MINGOTT

I know the one you mean. A stubborn, middle-class Englishman who came to the colonies with every intention of living for a bank account instead of dying for a creed.

[DELIA *looks a little startled*. MRS. MIN-
GOTT *adds quickly:*]

Don't look as if I'd said something against Jim, you
goose.

[*However, she continues bluntly, with the
air of being, as always, very sure of her
ground:*]

All our old families were not founded by gentlemen.
A great many people came to this country to get on,
and for no other reason. And they *have* got on.
That's why you married a Ralston, and why my
mother married one. And that's why they and their
kind have imposed their own rigid ideas on society
wherever they've settled and prospered.

[*Then more casually.*]

But you haven't told me yet how you managed to
change high tea into dinner in a Ralston household.

DELIA

[*Slyly.*]

Jim may have rigid opinions, but he *can* be persuaded. Even if he *is* a Ralston, he's still a man. And
when I wouldn't let him kiss me for two days, he
came round . . . Now he smiles at people who keep on
having dinner in the middle of the day, and says he
can't bear their narrow-mindedness.

MRS. MINGOTT

Do you know what I think about you, my dear
Delia? I think you're much wiser than you're suspected of being—even by people wiser than yourself.

DELIA

[*With her pretty, lazy smile, and a little shrug.*]

Do you?

[*Then anxiously.*]

I do hope Chatty will learn how to make Joe think he's having *his* own way. But he has a mind of his own, and she's very old-maidish in certain ways.

MRS. MINGOTT

[*Drily.*]

She's far from old-maidish in others.

[*Then reverting to the subject of* DELIA, *as she stares at her speculatively.*]

Yes, just how wise I don't know. But wise enough at any rate to have married my Ralston nephew instead of Clem Spender.

DELIA

[*Startled, softly.*]

Clem Spender!

MRS. MINGOTT

[*Significantly.*]

You see, I watched it all, from a distance.

DELIA

What—what was there to watch?

MRS. MINGOTT

A very pretty race between a tortoise and a hare. My nephew, Jim, used to write me about the pretty little Lovell girl; and my cousin Joe Spender's son, Clem, used to talk to me the winter I was in Italy about both the Lovell girls.

DELIA

Both?

MRS. MINGOTT

Yes, you were the one he was in love with, but he always had very pleasant things to say about Chatty, too ... Of course the tortoise won; but if I'd been a girl, the sterling virtues would have had no chance at all against Clem Spender.

DELIA

[*After an instant, in a low voice.*]
He's never been back since my marriage.
[*Then she fingers the trinket on the chain round her neck.*]
He brought me this. It's sweet, isn't it?
[*She takes it off and rises to show it to MRS. MINGOTT.*]
He knew I liked cameos. It's Psyche and Eros.

MRS. MINGOTT

[*Without enthusiasm.*]
Very pretty.

DELIA

[*Moving away, but staring for a moment at the cameo as she speaks quietly.*]
I've never told Jim that Clem gave it to me ... He doesn't like Clem. He used to say there was something cheap about him.

MRS. MINGOTT

I'm afraid there was. But as I said before, you're a wise young person.

[*Delia goes back to her chair, and sits down; but she forgets her embroidery.*]

DELIA

Then you think it was right for me to say nothing?

MRS. MINGOTT

It's always right for a woman not to say too much.

DELIA

[*After an instant.*]

Will he ever be a great painter?

MRS. MINGOTT

Clem? No; he's changed since his marriage to his rich cousin. They live in Rome, but I saw him in Paris not long ago. The spark's gone.

DELIA

[*Softly, more to herself than to* MRS. MINGOTT, *staring at the cameo.*]

Poor Clem . . . Poor dear boy . . .

[*There is a pause. Then* DELIA *takes up her embroidery, and* MRS. MINGOTT *lets her eyes close over the photographs.*

DR. LANSKELL *enters through the doorway at the back; he is a little exhilarated.*]

DR. LANSKELL

Oyster soup, broiled bass, stuffed goose, apple fritters, green peppers, and that famous caramel custard of your Grandmother Lovell's! That's what's considered pot-luck in this house, Mrs. Mingott. Even Joe's begun to brighten, and when he came in, I strongly suspected he'd settled into the gloom that comes over the happiest men when they see the altar just ahead of them.

DELIA

Dr. Lanskell!

> [*She laughs; then she looks at* MRS.
> MINGOTT, *whose eyes are opening slowly.*]

I'm afraid you're sleepy, Aunt Carrie.

MRS. MINGOTT
> [*Rallying at once.*]

I'm never sleepy.

DR. LANSKELL

Then couldn't we have some music?

DELIA

Isn't it too soon after dinner?

MRS. MINGOTT

Not for me.

DELIA

Do you still sing?

MRS. MINGOTT

Of course I still sing. I haven't lost my faculties.
> [*Rising.*]

Where's your instrument?

DELIA

[*Rising and leading the way into the next
room.*]

Here—

MRS. MINGOTT

[*As* DR. LANSKELL *stands aside to let
them pass.*]

Can you accompany me?

DELIA

Not very well, I'm afraid.

MRS. MINGOTT

Then I shall have to accompany myself.

[*Abruptly, almost accusingly, to* DR. LAN-
SKELL.]

You used to play for me.

DR. LANSKELL

Of course I did.

MRS. MINGOTT

Then come; I shall see whether or not you've let
yourself get rusty.

[*She precedes them into the next room.
Presently, after a waterfall of airy mel-
ody from the sweet, thin-toned spinet,*
MRS. MINGOTT *bursts into song...
Somewhere a bell is heard...* MRS.
MINGOTT *takes a high note and the
enterprise is going with sentimental bril-
liance when* CHARLOTTE *opens the door
from the hall and enters. She wears an*

ermine tippet over her cloak, and a fur
bonnet, and her face is spotted with the
bright color of inner excitement. She
halts, hearing the music. Flinging off her
cloak, she tiptoes to the threshold of the
next room, and signals. An instant later
DELIA *comes out.*]

DELIA
[*In amazement.*]

Chatty!

CHARLOTTE
[*Abruptly.*]

I had to see you. Can we talk here?

DELIA
[*With the blandness so characteristic of*
her and which never seems to desert her.]

Of course, darling. How handsome you look! I
always said you needed rich materials. This must be
one of your new cloaks. I'm so glad to see you out
of gray cashmere.

CHARLOTTE
[*Interrupting.*]

Can't you close that door?

DELIA
Yes; we might disturb Aunt Carrie, talking.

[*She goes and closes the door at the left.*
The room is suddenly still. She turns to
CHARLOTTE, *who stands nervously and*

*uncertainly back of a chair, clutching its
edge.*]

Now . . . But do take off your bonnet. It's very handsome and becoming, but it's heavy, I know. I've one
very like it for your wedding. I'll show it to you
later. I hope you like it; but it *is* heavy—

> [CHARLOTTE *is taking off her bonnet
> mechanically as* DELIA *prattles on.*]

Your hair seems lighter than it used to be, darling.

CHARLOTTE

> [*Suddenly realizing what* DELIA *is saying,
> and laughing shortly.*]

Lighter? It's gray. There—

> [*She lifts her hair from one temple; then
> she continues, with a twisted, tortured
> smile.*]

As for your bonnet—don't keep it for my wedding.
I may not be married.

DELIA

May not be married? Are you perfectly crazy?

CHARLOTTE

If it's crazy to do what I think right—

DELIA

Right! How can it be right to change your mind
now? You can't. Chatty, you simply can't!

> [*Then helplessly, as* CHARLOTTE'S *rigid
> attitude does not change.*]

What—what would people think?

CHARLOTTE

Oh—people!

[*She laughs shortly.*]

DELIA

What *is* the matter, Chatty? You look as if you'd seen an army of ghosts. You can't be well...

CHARLOTTE

[*Somberly.*]

I've seen Joe.

DELIA

Joe? Of course you've seen Joe. But...

[*Hesitantly.*]

Have you quarrelled? Is it something you've heard? Something in his past, perhaps—

CHARLOTTE

[*Interrupting blankly.*]

What *are* you talking about?

DELIA

[*A little foolishly.*]

Nothing definite. But I thought *you* must have heard something against him—to be so troubled.

CHARLOTTE

Oh, I see.

[*With an ironical smile.*]

No, I'd heard nothing against Joe; but if I had, I shouldn't be troubled, particularly. "Men will be men." And aren't to be judged too severely—as women are judged, for instance.

DELIA

[*With her bland common sense.*]

That's quite true. Men and women are different.

CHARLOTTE

[*Sharply.*]

Well, that's not it. It's nothing Joe's done.

DELIA

[*Uneasily.*]

What can be wrong, then? Tell me, Chatty. But don't keep standing. Sit down.

[CHARLOTTE *slumps into the chair.*]

CHARLOTTE

I want you to help me.

DELIA

Help you? How?

CHARLOTTE

With Joe. By saving us both from his Ralston ideas!

DELIA

The Ralston ideas? *I've* not found the Ralston ideas unbearable.

CHARLOTTE

No, but you wouldn't. And it was different with you. You weren't expected to give up things.

DELIA

What things? What is there for *you* to give up—?

CHARLOTTE

My poor children—he wants me to give *them* up!

DELIA

Of course he does, Chatty. Any man would.

CHARLOTTE

But I can't! I've told him I can't—

DELIA

So that's what Joe came to talk over with Jim! But Jim will think you ought to give them up, too.

CHARLOTTE

Naturally. They're two of a kind.

DELIA

But there really is the danger of disease, and if you have children of your own, you'd be exposing them—

CHARLOTTE

[*Interrupting.*]

Danger! Do you suppose there's really any danger? It's this everlasting Ralston cautiousness—this making mountains out of molehills—that I can't bear! Of course Joe's not always like the rest of them— pompous and crushing and solemn. If he were—I'd have known what to expect. But at that, he's not so different as I thought him.

DELIA

[*In a voice she seldom uses; which she keeps for emergencies.*]

You must try to be sensible, Chatty. Whether you agree with the Ralston ideas or not, you must realize that you'll never have another chance like this.

[*Then, after letting this sink into* CHARLOTTE'S *mind, in a different tone, lend-*

*ing herself, without real conviction, to
the* RALSTON *attitude.*]
After all, one's own babies have first claim.

CHARLOTTE

That's just it. How can I give up *my own baby?*

DELIA

[*Frightened, then taking account of* CHAR-
LOTTE'S *hysteria and finding refuge in a
pleasantry.*]
Yours—yours? Which of the poor waifs do you call
your own baby, my dear?

CHARLOTTE

[*Mercilessly, catching* DELIA'S *wrist.*]
I call my own baby *my own baby!*

DELIA

Your own—your own—? You're hurting my wrist,
Chatty—

CHARLOTTE

My own little girl—the one who lives with those
Negroes.

DELIA

Oh!

CHARLOTTE

The hundred-dollar baby! *She's* my own!

[*Then she releases* DELIA'S *hand and
covers her eyes with the back of her
wrist.*]

DELIA

Oh—poor Chatty! My poor Chatty!

> [CHARLOTTE *is crying suddenly.* DELIA *is still for an instant, unable to think; then suddenly, moved by pity, she puts her arm about* CHARLOTTE'S *shoulder, and speaks compassionately:*]

Chatty, tell me everything; don't look like that, darling!

CHARLOTTE

> [*In a dry voice; rising, and moving away.*]

What do you want me to tell you? That's all you need to know.

DELIA

I mean about yourself. Was it when you were in the South, after you were ill—?

> [*Then in a flash, understanding.*]

Or was that why you went South? Of course! That's why Dr. Lanskell sent you.

> [*With conviction.*]

He knew. But—but—

> [*Hesitantly; between curiosity and sympathy.*]

You loved someone—?

CHARLOTTE

> [*Harshly; standing in front of the fire, her back to* DELIA.]

Yes, but that's over.

DELIA

[*Almost afraid of her own thoughts, uncertainly.*]

But—it wasn't Joe you loved?

CHARLOTTE

Not then.

DELIA

But now?

CHARLOTTE

[*Wanly.*]

Oh yes . . . now . . . That's why I want to marry him. Because I love him. Not—

[*Bitterly.*]

—because he's a Ralston. Not even because I thought I'd have money for my baby—so she'd never have to be sent to an institution . . . Even that's not all. I should have loved *his* children too. As you said once, life doesn't stop. One gets lonely. One wants a home of one's own.

DELIA

I understand.

[*Then tenderly, helplessly, as* CHARLOTTE *comes back and drops down upon the sofa beside her.*]

Poor Chatty . . .

CHARLOTTE

[*Brokenly.*]

But I can't give up my baby, can I?

DELIA

No, no; of course not—

> [*At the sympathy in* DELIA'S *voice,* CHAR-
> LOTTE *gives way to tears again, her face
> in the crook of her arm on Delia's lap.*]

DELIA

> [*Repeating, as she strokes* CHARLOTTE'S
> *hair.*]

Of course not; we must think of some way—

CHARLOTTE

> [*Through her sobs.*]

If you could talk to Jim ... You can make Jim do
what you like—and if he could talk to Joe—and
persuade him that no harm can come of my going
on with my nursery—

DELIA

Don't cry like that. I'll do my best to help you, one
way or another.

CHARLOTTE

Oh, Delia, if only you can!

DELIA

> [*After an instant, but not very hopefully.*]

If you could tell Joe—

CHARLOTTE

> [*Lifting her head, sitting up very straight.*]

I couldn't. He'd never forgive me. He must never
know.

DELIA

No; you are right. You couldn't tell Joe. But—

[*Recovering her poise sufficiently to try to
cope with the situation, but hesitating to
remind* CHARLOTTE *of memories which
must be painful.*]

—We're talking as if—as if—you didn't have to—to
consider the—the person who—who took advantage
of you. After all, he's your child's father.

CHARLOTTE

[*Drily, but with sudden reserve.*]

No one took advantage of me. I was lonely and
unhappy. He was lonely and unhappy.... Besides,
he never thought of marrying me ... People don't
all have your luck ... But, even if he had wanted to
marry me, mamma would never have consented.
And so—one day before he went away—

DELIA

[*As she stops suddenly.*]

He went away?

CHARLOTTE

Yes.

DELIA

Knowing?

CHARLOTTE

What was going to happen? No. I didn't know myself, then.

DELIA

But afterwards?

CHARLOTTE

No, never. He never knew. He never came back.

DELIA

But shouldn't he have known? After all—

CHARLOTTE

[*Impatiently, as* DELIA *pauses.*]

Why? He couldn't have helped me. He was in no
position to marry anyone. Besides, he didn't love me.
He loved someone else.

DELIA

[*Abruptly.*]

Where did he go?

CHARLOTTE

[*Evasively.*]

Oh, what does it matter? You wouldn't understand—

DELIA

You won't tell me who it was?

CHARLOTTE

Why should I? I've never told anybody.

DELIA

How can I help you if you don't trust me?

CHARLOTTE

[*After an instant, stubbornly.*]

Haven't I told you all you need to know?

DELIA

[*Her voice hard with suspicion.*]

Where did he go—out of the country—? To—to
Italy?

CHARLOTTE

Oh!

[*She flings an arm across her eyes;* DELIA
*rises; then, as if unable to stand, sits
down again.*]

DELIA

[*At last.*]

Then it *was* to Italy . . . It was Clem Spender!

[*All compassion has gone from her face;
her eyes narrow.*]

CHARLOTTE

[*Humbly, covering her face with her
hands to avoid* DELIA'S *eyes.*]

I told you he loved somebody else . . . It was because
you hadn't waited for him—

DELIA

[*Rising at last.*]

Stop!

[*The single word is both a command and
a cry. Then she moves away as if she
could not bear having* CHARLOTTE *near
her.*]

CHARLOTTE

[*Bitterly.*]

I knew it! I knew you'd not forgive *that*. But you've
got to listen now!

[*Then in an uneven voice.*]

I'd been in love with him ever since I was a girl. He
seemed everything that was romantic to me. But he
never even looked at anybody but you, until that time
—at your wedding, when you'd asked me to look

after him. Then he began coming to me for sympathy. And I was so sorry for him; I loved him so much—

[*She breaks off.*]

DELIA

[*Scornfully.*]

Oh, Chatty, how could you? How could you—when he didn't even pretend to love you!

CHARLOTTE

I shouldn't have told you! I knew you'd not understand—

DELIA

You are right. I don't understand. Though I could if it had been someone who really loved you, or who you thought loved you. But hadn't you any pride at all?

CHARLOTTE

[*Her eyes narrowing; and her own voice growing hard.*]

You needn't be so contemptuous. I've never been sorry . . . not really sorry . . .

DELIA

[*After an instant, recovering her composure; coldly.*]

And he's never known about the child?

CHARLOTTE

No. Why should he? It's nobody's business but mine. Besides, that's over—all over . . . There's nothing left of anything I ever felt for him—except my baby.

DELIA

[*As if to a stranger.*]

But why did you come to me? What did you expect
me to do for you?

CHARLOTTE

[*Wearily.*]

Must we go over all that again? I came because I
can't marry Joe if it means giving up my child.

[*With a bitter ironic smile.*]

Have you forgotten you were going to help me, so
soon?

DELIA

But, after all, what can *I* do?

CHARLOTTE

[*Impatiently.*]

What the man you loved would have wanted you
to do!

DELIA

[*In a hard voice.*]

What do you think he'd have wanted me to do!

CHARLOTTE

[*Somberly.*]

If Joe were Clem, and I asked *him* if I might go on
caring for these poor children, he'd laugh and call
me a goose, and wonder why I bothered to ask such
a question.

DELIA

[*Also somberly; more to herself than to
CHARLOTTE.*]

Yes, that would be Clem Spender's way. He'd always do the generous thing, even if it meant that others would have to pay the score.

CHARLOTTE

[*As if she has hardly noticed* DELIA'S *comment, in her preoccupation with her own thoughts.*]

But if you can't persuade Joe that I should be permitted to go to my nursery every day, so I can see my own baby and watch over her, you can at least help me to get out of this marriage as decently as possible without hurting him.

DELIA

[*Harshly.*]

Do you think it's not hurting Joe to marry him, with such a secret on your conscience?

CHARLOTTE

[*Stubbornly.*]

What he doesn't know—what no one knows—can't hurt him.

DELIA

[*Insistently.*]

But suppose you do marry him, and he finds it out?

CHARLOTTE

I made up my mind a long time ago to risk that—though it's the reason I held him off so long. But I'll make it up in other ways—for deceiving him. He'll not be sorry he married me, Delia.

DELIA

[*Harshly.*]

But you don't love him as much as you once loved Clem Spender.

CHARLOTTE

I love him—*differently.* As you love Jim, differently, perhaps.

[*Then humbly.*]

And I need Joe's love—

> [*She breaks off as* DELIA *turns her eyes away, and then continues passionately.*]

Oh, I can imagine what you think of me! But if I choose to deceive him, it's not your business, it's mine.

DELIA

> [*After an instant, in a hard, troubled voice.*]

I don't know what to say. I can't think. You must give me time.

CHARLOTTE

[*Almost spent.*]

There *is* no time. I must decide—now—tonight—and I can't think—either—

> [*She presses her hands to her head; then she rises abruptly and picks up her cloak and bonnet.*]

DELIA

[*Coldly, almost indifferently.*]

Where are you going?

CHARLOTTE

I don't know ... I want to walk—to be out in the air. I think I want to be alone—

DELIA

[*Making a decision; sharply, as to a child.*]

Go upstairs, to my room—and wait. Joe's here, with Jim, now. I'll try to do what I think best.

CHARLOTTE

[*Desperately.*]

Do *something!* Whatever you do, you can't make things worse.

DELIA

Whatever happens, that child shan't stay with those Negroes. I do promise you *that*.

CHARLOTTE

[*A light coming into her face.*]

You promise that? You do promise—? To save her?

DELIA

Yes; but I must manage it in my own way. Will you wait? Or shall I send for a coach to take you home now, and see you tomorrow?

CHARLOTTE

[*After an instant, drawing a sharp breath of decision.*]

I'll wait.

[*Then, dragging her cloak over her arm, looking neither to the left nor to the right, and not trusting herself to say more, she goes to the door at the back, opens it, and goes out, closing it behind her. Left alone,* DELIA *walks the length of the room and back, agitated by her memories, her jealousy, and the need for action of some sort in behalf of* CHAR-LOTTE.]

JAMES *and* JOSEPH *enter from the room where* MRS. MINGOTT *is now singing a duet with* DR. LANSKELL, *letting the sound of spinet and voices in with them, and then closing them out with the soft, cautious closing of the door.* DELIA *would prefer not to see them at this instant, but they are delighted at finding her alone. She drops into a chair on the far side of the table and takes up her embroidery.]*

JAMES

[*With the optimism of one who has dined very well.*]

This is luck; here's Delia now; all by herself. So go ahead, my boy, and tell her the whole story before Aunt Carrie exhausts her repertoire—and Dr. Lanskell.

[*He laughs at his little joke; then with a solicitous look at* DELIA *at finding her unresponsive:*]

You look a little pale, my dear.

Delia

[*Rigidly.*]

It's nothing.

James

[*Seating himself; trying to create an atmosphere of intimacy; to* Joseph.]

Take that chair.

[*As* Joseph *sits.*]

Now we can talk comfortably.

[*To* Delia.]

Joe has something on his mind that I've advised him to consult you about.

Delia

[*Looking up from her embroidery; managing to keep her voice even.*]

I think I know what it is. Chatty's been here.

Joseph

[*Anxiously.*]

Then she's told you? Is she angry?

Delia

She—she's very unhappy. She can't understand why you don't want her to go on with the nursery after your marriage. And of course

[*With an undercurrent of meaning.*]

you can't understand why she wants to.

Joseph

I admit it. I can't!

James

Nobody can.

JOSEPH

And that's what I've tried to tell her, that people will think it odd, if she does.

DELIA

[*With a kind of bitterness, still in the same taut voice.*]

Charlotte's never cared very much for what other people think. If she had—

[*She stops abruptly.*]

JOSEPH

[*With unwilling admiration.*]

That's true. She feels it her duty to go on giving these waifs her personal attention. She doesn't even mind being thought eccentric—or laughed at, even—because of her—her excessive zeal, in their behalf.

DELIA

[*Sharply.*]

Well then, why not let her be laughed at if *she* doesn't mind? Why do you put the question to me?

JAMES

I advised him to, my dear.

JOSEPH

Yes; Jim knows that I've come to have great respect for your judgment. We all have, in fact. Every member of our family now looks to you to decide important issues. So I want you to say if I'm wrong in not wanting Chatty to spend several hours a day with these children, whom we don't know, who

came from heaven knows where, and who have no
possible claim on her. I want you to tell me if I'm
obstinate, as she seems to think, or if I *am* right.

JAMES

[*Flatly.*]

Of course you're right, and Chatty ought to realize
it.

DELIA

[*Bending over her embroidery; without encour-
agement.*]

Right or wrong, Joe, you'll find that Chatty won't
give in.

JOSEPH

[*Insistently, after an instant.*]

But if you spoke to her? She must respect your opin-
ion, too, couldn't you make her see that I'm not
being narrow-minded or dictatorial? That I'm really
thinking only of her?

DELIA

I've never had any influence over Charlotte, and
I'd have none now.

JOSEPH

But surely she'd listen to *you*—if you told her—

DELIA

[*Nervously, sharply.*]

No. No, she wouldn't.

[*Looking up, at last; not displeased because there seems no chance of an agree-*

ment between CHARLOTTE *and* JOSEPH
on this subject. Continuing, with con-
viction.]

I'm afraid it's no use. I'm afraid none of us can
persuade her to give up those paupers she's so attached to.

JAMES
[*Rising, impatiently.*]

But surely she can't be more attached to them than
to the man she's going to marry!

DELIA
[*Shrugging.*]

It's a different thing entirely. You must have noticed how fond she is of that little girl we saw today,
for instance.

JOSEPH
[*More impersonally, after an instant; try-*
ing to be fair.]

Yes, I understand that. But why shouldn't she go on
being interested in them, and fond of them, even,
without giving them so much of her time and herself?

[*Then impulsively, as* DELIA *makes no*
effort to answer.]

I've told her I'm willing to give her whatever she
needs for them. God! I'm willing to draw up a
paper to that effect before a lawyer if she wants
me to.

DELIA

[*Really surprised.*]

That's very generous of you, Joe.

JAMES

[*Explosively.*]

Generous! It's unheard of.

>[*He stops pacing back of the table between
>DELIA and JOSEPH, and sits down
>again.*]

DELIA

>[*Continuing evenly, as if JAMES had not
>spoken; watching JOSEPH out of the cor-
>ners of her eyes.*]

But it's not enough.

JOSEPH

>[*Still trying to look at the matter from
>CHARLOTTE'S point of view.*]

No; I suppose it isn't. What she's set her heart on is
giving them her personal care; she wants to go to
her nursery every day, herself. That's what it boils
down to.

>[*Reluctantly.*]

And I'd let her. I really would. I'd stretch a point and
give her her own way, for the time being, and put
up with the inconvenience of having her away from
home so much, if there weren't a much more seri-
ous reason.

DELIA
[*Lifting her head.*]
What is that?

JOSEPH
Her health.

DELIA
Her health?

JOSEPH
I can speak to you frankly, Delia, as my brother's
wife.
[*Reluctantly.*]
You—you know the apprehensions that certain rela-
tives of ours have entertained on that score?

DELIA
Because Chatty was sent South that time, you mean?

JOSEPH
Yes; and because her father died young. So I put
the question to you, fairly and squarely: in the cir-
cumstances am I foolishly apprehensive? Or should
Chatty be permitted to go on taking unnecessary
risks?

DELIA
[*Refusing to take* CHARLOTTE'S *part; still
agitated by her secret.*]
I don't know. I can't say. Perhaps in her place I'd
feel just as she does. In any case, I can't advise her.
Or you. I can't interfere . . .
[*Then coolly.*]
But since it seems to be a matter of deciding between

you and these miserable children, I don't know what
you can do if she chooses them, except . . .

> [*She pauses, leaving her implication in the
> air.*]

JOSEPH

> [*After an instant, abruptly, unexpectedly.*]

If she choose them, it's because she thinks she's
doing what is right. And in that case, *I* must be the
one to give in.

JAMES

Don't tell me you're going to let her have her own
way, after all!

JOSEPH

> [*As* DELIA *stares.*]

Yes. Nothing's important enough to come between
us now.

DELIA

> [*Sharply, unbelievingly.*]

You mean you've really decided that Chatty is to
do exactly as she likes, in this matter?

JOSEPH

> [*Decisively.*]

Exactly as she likes, so long as she doesn't overtax
her strength; and I'm going to tell her so, at once.

> [*He rises.*]

DELIA

No! It's no use!

JOSEPH

What?

DELIA

It's no use. You were talking just now about her health—saying what we all know—that the Ralstons weren't eager to have you choose a wife who wasn't strong, and who might—

[*She breaks off, and then continues, her voice rising.*]

It's no use, I tell you. Chatty *can't* marry you. She can't marry anyone now.

JOSEPH

[*Blankly.*]

I don't understand you.

DELIA

She's ill. Chatty's ill again. She coughed blood here, in this room, a minute ago.

[JAMES *rises, profoundly shocked.* DELIA *continues, sharply, nervously; to* JOSEPH:]

You know what that means. She can't marry anyone, I tell you!

JAMES

[*As* JOSEPH *stares at* DELIA, *unable to speak.*]

My God! But you know you've got to buck up, old boy!

JOSEPH

[*Unsteadily.*]

But—why—why wasn't I told at once?

DELIA

[*Unnerved by the feeling he has shown.*]

Because such—such things aren't easy to tell.

> [*Suddenly she drops her head down at the
> table, covering her face with her hands.*]

JAMES

[*Sympathetically, but not losing his head
as he is afraid* JOSEPH *is doing.*]

Delia's right, you know. If poor Chatty's ill again,
marriage isn't to be thought of. Better face the
music now than later. Better get it over with—

JOSEPH

> [*Blinking away the tears that come to
> his eyes.*]

But I—I can't give her up. I can't—!

JAMES

> [*Grimly.*]

You can't marry her now; that's certain.

JOSEPH

I must see her. Where is she?

DELIA

> [*Rises.*]

You must let me see her first. I must tell her I've
told you. This is hard for her too, you know, and
you must be tactful and wait until she sends for
you.

> [*The door opens and* DR. LANSKELL *en-
> ters unexpectedly; all three turn at the
> interruption.*]

DR. LANSKELL

The concert is over.

DELIA

Where's Aunt Carrie?

DR. LANSKELL

She went up. She asked me to say good-night for her. I gather that you're discussing something important; so I'm going to slip away too.

JOSEPH
[*In a harsh, tense voice.*]

Dr. Lanskell—

DR. LANSKELL
[*Arrested.*]

Yes?

JOSEPH

When Chatty went South six years ago of a lung disease, she was expected to die as her father did, wasn't she?

DR. LANSKELL
[*After a strained instant; trying to speak casually.*]

I thought everyone knew that, Joe. Didn't you?

JOSEPH
[*In the same tense voice.*]

That disease is in her family, isn't it?

DR. LANSKELL

Everyone knows that, too.

JOSEPH

What if Chatty weren't cured? What if it should come back?

DR. LANSKELL

[*Frankly troubled.*]

Why do you ask me that? Isn't Chatty perfectly well?

JOSEPH

[*Insistently.*]

Because I want you to say whether she should marry or not, if she began coughing blood again.

DR. LANSKELL

Has Chatty coughed blood?

JOSEPH

Yes. What do you say to *that?*

DR. LANSKELL

That it's a very bad sign.

JOSEPH

That's all. Good-night.

[*He strides towards the door, his face averted.*]

JAMES

Wait—old man—don't go like this! I'll walk along with you.

JOSEPH

I'd rather you didn't. Thanks for your kindness, both of you.

[*Then he is gone; but* JAMES *follows him out, closing the door after him.*]

DR. LANSKELL

[*Quietly; looking at* DELIA *searchingly.*]

I don't understand at all. Chatty's stronger than most young women. When did this happen?

DELIA

[*Softly, in a low voice, with a cautious glance towards the closed doors.*]

Dr. Lanskell, Chatty didn't go South because of her lungs.

DR. LANSKELL

[*Again taken by surprise.*]

Well?

DELIA

I know why she went.

DR. LANSKELL

[*Looking at her sternly.*]

Well?

DELIA

That's why she musn't marry Joe. Not because she's ill.

DR. LANSKELL

Isn't she?

DELIA

No.

DR. LANSKELL

[*After an instant.*]

Who decided that? Did she?

DELIA

No. *I* did.

DR. LANSKELL

With or without her consent?

DELIA

[*Faltering a little.*]

Without.

DR. LANSKELL

[*Sharply.*]

You've taken a great deal on yourself, Delia Lovell.

DELIA

[*Quickly.*]

You think I've done wrong?

DR. LANSKELL

I think it's a sacrilegious thing to lay so much as a finger on another person's destiny.

DELIA

But she came to me herself, to beg me to help her— so she wouldn't have to give up her child. This was the only way. I *wouldn't* help her deceive Joe. I wouldn't connive at a lie, like that. Not to Jim's brother.

DR. LANSKELL

Well?

DELIA

But I feel that I can make it up to her by caring for her child. I'm going to take the little girl, myself.

DR. LANSKELL

[*Again sharply.*]

Chatty's little girl?

DELIA

Chatty's and Clem Spender's. You see, I know everything.

DR. LANSKELL

If you're counting on me to back you up in this lie, I will make one condition.

DELIA

What is it?

DR. LANSKELL

That you're not to take Chatty's child from her.

DELIA

But it's the only way—and after all, if she could give her to Negroes, she should be willing to give her to me.

DR. LANSKELL

Most of you have forgotten that Jessamine, the Negress who found the child on her door-step, was Chatty's nurse when she was a little girl. Chatty knew she could trust her.

DELIA

But I intend to give the child a proper home, where Chatty can come and see her as often as she likes.

DR. LANSKELL

You must find a way to let Chatty keep her child for herself.

DELIA

But—

DR. LANSKELL

No doubt you mean well, my dear, but each of us

has the right to love and suffer, to lie or to tell the truth, after his own fashion. And now that Charlotte has put herself at your mercy in telling you her secret—be generous to her. Don't make her your enemy through a mistaken sense of duty. Above all, don't try to take from her the one thing which is really her own ... I won't wait for Jim ... Goodnight.

> [*He turns to go.*]

DELIA

> . [*Uncertainly.*]

Dr. Lanskell—

> [*He turns back.*]

DR. LANSKELL

Yes?

DELIA

> [*Quietly.*]

You are right. I have done a sacrilegious thing. Deliberately.

DR. LANSKELL

> [*Impressed by her frankness.*]

Doubtless you felt that you were in the right.

DELIA

> [*Unhappily.*]

It may not be to my credit, if I was.

DR. LANSKELL

The wisest of us make mistakes. And sometimes we never learn whether or not they *were* mistakes. I hope yours wasn't.

[*Then he turns and goes through the door
at the back.* DELIA *looks at the cameo
she wears, with conflicting emotions. An
instant later* JAMES *enters from the next
room, carrying a small tray on which
there are a decanter of brandy and three
small glasses.*]

JAMES
[*Filling a glass.*]
Joe sent me back; he's hard hit, poor fellow. He'll
probably go away somewhere, alone, for a while . . .
I thought you might need a drop of brandy, after
all you've been through. But where's—?

DELIA
[*Interrupting, nervously.*]
Dr. Lanskell? Gone.
[*As he offers her a glass, she refuses it
by a gesture, turning away from him.*]

JAMES
[*His glance following her, proudly.*]
I'm not sorry he's left us alone.
[*He swallows the brandy and sets the glass
on a table. Then he continues, going to
her, and putting his arms about her.*]
I never admired you more than tonight, darling . . .
My wise Delia.
[*She lets him kiss her, then draws away.*]

DELIA

What should you have done, Jim, if I'd had to tell
you about myself what I told Joe about Chatty?

JAMES

[*Frowning away the question as absurd.*]
I can't think.

DELIA

[*Moving away, and dropping down on the
sofa, in front of the fire.*]
Poor Chatty—nothing left now.

JAMES

Lucky now she has those paupers, isn't it? I suppose a woman *must* have children to love—somebody else's if not her own.

[*He comes and sits beside her.*]

DELIA

[*Craftily, as she leans against his shoulder.*]
Yes, I see no other happiness for her. You know,
darling—

[*As if with an inspiration.*]
—you and I should see that she keeps her babies.

JAMES

But suppose she's sent away—to the South, again?

DELIA

She may not get worse immediately. And if she
isn't, may I tell her that you and I will see that
she has money for her nursery, so she won't have to

beg of grandmamma? I could give it to her out of my pin-money?

JAMES

Not from your pin-money! Never! But as much as you want from me for Chatty and her paupers.

DELIA

Dearest!

[*She sinks back into his arms, and responds to his kiss. Then after an instant she speaks again; beguilingly:*]

We might even manage to let her take that little girl —the one she's grown so fond of, to live with her in a place of her own; couldn't we manage that?

JAMES

I don't see why not, if Chatty would like it.

DELIA

Oh, she would! I know she would.

[*With her cheek against his; intimately.*]

When I think of our own precious . . .

JAMES

Let's go up—

DELIA

[*Drawing away again.*]

You go, dearest. And send Chatty down. I didn't tell you, but she's still here.

JAMES

Here?

DELIA

Waiting to hear what I've said to Joe. Send her
down, and I'll come up as soon as she's gone.

JAMES

Very well.

DELIA

[*As they rise, and she strolls with him
towards the door at the back.*]
And whatever you do, don't mention her illness to
her tonight.

JAMES

No, dearest, if you tell me not to. But steady yourself with a sip of that brandy.

[*Then, bending for a last kiss, he hurries
from the room, leaving the door to the
hall open, and disappears up the stairs.
DELIA pours a little brandy into a glass,
but does not drink it . . . CHARLOTTE
comes running down the stairs into the
room, closing the door behind her. She
tosses her cloak and bonnet upon a
chair.*]

CHARLOTTE

Delia? Jim said you wanted me.

[*Her breath comes fast.*]

DELIA

[*Holding out the glass.*]
Drink it, darling; it'll do you good.

CHARLOTTE

No . . . Tell me quickly, or I shall know that what's coming is too dreadful!

DELIA

[*Setting the glass down, untouched, and studying* CHARLOTTE'S *eager face a moment before beginning.*]

You can't marry Joe, dear—can you—and keep little Tina?

CHARLOTTE

Not keep her with me, no; but I could be with her every day, at the nursery for the present; and afterwards—

[*Vaguely, hopefully.*]

—make her a home somewhere where I could slip away to see her, I hope—

DELIA

[*In a flat voice.*]

See your own child in secret? Always in dread of disgrace? And risks of all sorts to your husband and your other children? Haven't you thought of the danger there'd be?

CHARLOTTE

No, I can't think—I've not been able to think that far ahead!

[*Then, desperately.*]

You're trying to tell me that I must give her up.

DELIA

No. Only that you must not marry Joe.

CHARLOTTE

[*Blankly.*]

What—?

DELIA

I promised to help you, didn't I? I promised I wouldn't let the child stay with those blacks? But I didn't promise that you should marry Joe, too. Well —I've done the best I could . . . You and little Tina shall be together, always.

CHARLOTTE

[*Quickly.*]

But Joe?

[*In a sick voice.*]

You didn't tell him—? I couldn't bear that! What *did* you tell him?

DELIA

That you were coughing blood again.

CHARLOTTE

[*After a long startled pause; shuddering.*]

Oh Delia. . . ! How could you?

DELIA

[*Smoothly.*]

I had to tell him something.

[*Then, as the storm gathers in* CHAR-LOTTE'S *face; forcefully.*]

If you were to keep your child, the engagement had to be broken.

CHARLOTTE

[*Bitterly.*]

So you frightened him away. I see!

DELIA

He's dreadfully unhappy, of course, but he accepts your decision—

CHARLOTTE

[*Ironically.*]

My decision!

DELIA

Well, *mine* then.

CHARLOTTE

But if *I* don't accept your decision—? If I tell him the truth?

DELIA

I thought you couldn't bear to have him know the truth.

CHARLOTTE

But if I should tell him, and he should say he'd forgive me—!

DELIA

If there'd been any hope of that, would you have come to me?

CHARLOTTE

No; but you drive me to think of such follies—

DELIA

Give up follies, Charlotte; and try to realize what it's going to mean to you to make a home for your

child. That's what you wanted most, isn't it? To
have her with you, and take care of her yourself?

CHARLOTTE

[*Desperately.*]

Yes—but—

DELIA

[*Impatiently; in a tone of finality.*]

Well, I've done what I could. I've made Jim promise
to give you a little house of your own and arrange
for Tina to live with you. I can't do more; and if
you're not satisfied, I must wash my hands of both
of you. Unless you're sensible now, *I can do nothing for you or your child.* Remember that.

> [CHARLOTTE *goes to the window and
> stands, considering a long moment. Then
> she turns back, and speaks at last;
> brokenly.*]

CHARLOTTE

You said—together always—Tina and I . . . ?

DELIA

Yes. I said you should have Tina with you always.

CHARLOTTE

Just ourselves?

DELIA

Just yourselves.

CHARLOTTE

In a little house of our own?

DELIA

Yes.

CHARLOTTE

You're sure, Delia?

DELIA

Quite sure, dearest. Jim has promised because he thinks you're ill and we don't want you to be lonely.

[*Then, as* DELIA *waits,* CHARLOTTE, *crying softly, catches up one of the skeins of bright silk which lie with* DELIA'S *embroidery on the table, and drawing* JOE'S *ring from her finger, slips the threads through it; for an instant she stands, still hesitating, letting the ring swing from her hand. Then suddenly she tosses it upon the table, and without looking at* DELIA, *turns to gather up her cloak and bonnet, as the curtain falls.*]

FOURTH EPISODE
1853

Fourteen years later. A winter evening.

The same room, which looks different, however, because the movables are now of the Victorian instead of the late Empire style.

CHARLOTTE, looking much more than fourteen years older, has passed into a different generation; wearing a severely plain dress, she sits near the fire, knitting. Her hair, now gray, is drawn tightly back from her colorless face in which even her once fine eyes and bright lips have grown indistinct; and she is the typical old maid in appearance as well as manner; harsh, and inclined to be tyrannical . . . DR. LANSKELL sits near her, but the passage of fourteen years seems, by contrast, to have changed him very little; although when he walks it is with a slower step, and he is more likely to nod in a comfortable chair by a warm fire after dinner.

Again there is singing in the next room; but the quartet of voices is accompanied on the new piano instead of on the old spinet.

Presently the music softens; and Charlotte speaks abruptly

CHARLOTTE

It's very good of you to sit here and keep me company when you might be with Delia and her young people ... You always liked singing, I remember.

DR. LANSKELL

I still do. And Tina and young Delia both have very pretty voices. But they like the new songs and I know only the old ones.

CHARLOTTE

[*After an instant.*]

Lanning Halsey brought the latest ones back from Paris with him. And there's always music in the house since he came.

DR. LANSKELL

[*Refusing to recognize the complaint underlying her words.*]

That must be very pleasant for everyone.

[CHARLOTTE *says nothing. The music continues.*

A young woman is seen through the open doorway at the back, coming down the stairs. She is DELIA'S *married daughter,* "DEE" HALSEY, *and she is twenty years old. She wears an evening dress, and flowers in her hair. She enters the room with a light, quick step and lays a scarf about* CHARLOTTE'S *shoulders. When she speaks, her voice is fresh and sweet,*

and she seems unspoiled, self-possessed,
and mature for her age.]

DEE

Here's your scarf, Cousin Chatty.

CHARLOTTE

[*Gratefully.*]

Thank you, Dee.

[*Then querulously.*]

I thought I asked Tina to fetch it.

DEE

But I knew she'd forget; she and mamma are trying
some new songs with Lanning and John.

[*Then lifting her head, listening, as the*
song ends.]

That one's pretty, isn't it?

DR. LANSKELL

Very.

CHARLOTTE

[*Ungraciously.*]

You'll be late for your ball unless you start soon.

DEE

[*With a laugh.*]

I know; but Tina and Lanning simply won't be
hurried. However, I'll try again.

[*She goes into the next room. But someone*
has begun to try a new piece on the
piano, and continues to grope tonelessly
through its unfamiliar passages, while
one thin, pretty voice hums the air.

DR. LANSKELL

[*Resuming their conversation; in an optimistic vein.*]

In fact, when you consider how pleasant life is in this house, for young Tina particularly, you must feel a deep satisfaction in having managed to give her such a home.

CHARLOTTE

[*Drily.*]

If Tina's life has been pleasant in this house, it's Delia who's made it so; not I.

DR. LANSKELL

[*Kindly.*]

We won't talk of your own sacrifices for the child, Chatty; but Delia's done her best, too.

CHARLOTTE

[*In a passion of resentment.*]

Her best to spoil her—from the day she brought us here to live, after Jim's death twelve years ago! And now that Delia's own girl is married, there's nothing —nothing at all—that Tina doesn't have, or can't have, by asking for it.

[*As though there were no point in saying anything further,* DR. LANSKELL *gets up. At the same instant the person playing the piano breaks off abruptly, and a murmur of talk and laughter precedes the group coming from the next room into this.*]

CHARLOTTE

[*To* DR. LANSKELL, *in a more agreeable tone.*]

You're not going?

DR. LANSKELL

Yes; I must look in on one of my patients on my way home, and it's getting late.

[*Indicating a pill-box on the table.*]

This is for Delia, in case her headache comes back. Good-night.

[*Charlotte rises.*]

CHARLOTTE

Good-night, Dr. Lanskell.

[*As he turns to go,* DELIA *enters through the doorway at the left, between* TINA *and* DEE, *followed by* LANNING *and* JOHN HALSEY. DELIA *is still rosy and fair, and she and* TINA *move forward with arms entwined round each other's waist.* DEE *falls behind with* JOHN, *her husband; and* LANNING, *with rather a lordly air, comes last. They surround* DR. LANSKELL, *who is already on his way out through the doorway at the back, and has no intention of being detained.*]

DELIA

Oh, are you going?

DR. LANSKELL

Yes, I must; good-night, all of you.

TINA *and* DEE

[*Answering at same time.*]

Good-night, Dr. Lanskell—

Good-night—

LANNING

[*Also at the same time.*]

Good-night, sir—

JOHN

I'll help you with your coat—

DELIA

Good-night; thank you for coming; but I wish you'd been in time for dinner—

> [*He pats her on the arm, and goes, fol-*
> *lowed by* JOHN, *into the entrance pas-*
> *sage beyond.*]

CHARLOTTE

> [*Ungraciously, as she sits down again, and*
> *the others stroll forward; with a sharp*
> *glance at* TINA.]

The carriage has been waiting twenty minutes, and the horses don't like standing a cold night like this.

> [*Everyone begins to answer at once.*]

DELIA

> [*Holding up her hand for order.*]

They're going now.

TINA

Yes; we're just going.

[JOHN *returns.*]

LANNING

It doesn't matter if we're late, at a ball.

JOHN

[*Good-naturedly.*]

Being late *anywhere* matters more than you think.
[*Quoting.*]

"Punctuality is the virtue of Kings," you know.

CHARLOTTE

[*Drily; not looking up from her knitting, which she has taken up again.*]

And it's not unbecoming to anyone to make a habit of being on time.

LANNING

[*Airily, as he and* TINA *smile at each other.*]

I know. "The early bird catches the worm." "Take care of the pennies and the pounds will take care of themselves." "There's a rainy day coming." "What's worth doing at all is worth doing well—"

[TINA *laughs, rather too loudly.*]

CHARLOTTE

[*Reprovingly.*]

Tina!

[TINA *shrugs, and makes a little grimace which* CHARLOTTE *doesn't see, and which makes* LANNING *laugh in turn. Again* CHARLOTTE *looks up, and fixing him with her glance, continues severely:*]

CHARLOTTE

I see nothing to laugh at. Your cousin's right, Lanning.

LANNING

[*Teasingly.*]

As usual.

CHARLOTTE

[*In the same severe tone.*]

Yes, as usual.

LANNING

And I'm wrong, as usual.

CHARLOTTE

Yes. John knows that people who have no regard for punctuality usually have no regard for other things.

TINA

[*Speaking for the first time; in a tone of protest.*]

Cousin Chatty!

CHARLOTTE

[*Looking at her with somber eyes.*]

You might have a little more yourself. You're often late.

TINA

[*Again with a shrug and grimace.*]

Cousin Chatty's always finding fault with me!

CHARLOTTE

[*Gravely; again busy with her knitting.*]

You're not perfection, my child.

TINA

I know I'm not perfect—but—

LANNING

Who is?

DEE *and* JOHN
[*At the same moment, looking at each other.*]

John is—
Dee is—

[*Even* CHARLOTTE *smiles as the others laugh outright.*]

TINA
[*As the laughter subsides.*]

But you've not been married a year yet. Wait!

DEE
[*Quickly, but with perfect friendliness.*]

We'll not wait for you until one o'clock again to-night, Scatterbrain; and if you've disappeared when we're ready to go, you'll have to find someone else to see you home.

JOHN

Delia knows I have to be at the bank early, and I'm no good if I don't have my sleep. And two nights last week you weren't to be found.

TINA
[*Not entirely pleased by this as* CHAR-LOTTE *again lifts her head, listening.*]

But both times I thought you'd gone on. I'd told you the Vandergraves would bring me.

CHARLOTTE

[*Harshly.*]

You went with Dee and John; and should have been ready to leave with them. It's not the Vandergraves' duty to see you home.

TINA

But they live next door, Cousin Chatty—and there's always room in their carriage.

DELIA

[*Mildly; disliking to reprove* TINA.]

I expected you to come with Dee, my dear. I'm sorry, John.

> [*Then quickly, to change the subject; to the two girls.*]

Run on up, now, and put on your things.

DEE

I'm going.

> [*As she disappears through the doorway at the back, and up the stairs.*]

Come along, Tina! Get ready, John.

TINA

> [*Reluctantly to* DELIA, *as* JOHN *also disappears, followed by* LANNING.]

I do wish you were coming, too, mamma; Cousin Chatty doesn't mind being alone—

DELIA

But this is a young people's ball, darling.

TINA

You're young.

CHARLOTTE

[*Harshly.*]

Stop your teasing, Tina, and go and get ready.

> [TINA *again makes a little grimace to* DELIA, *behind* CHARLOTTE'S *back, but makes no move to go.*]

TINA

[*Sitting on the arm of* DELIA'S *chair.*]

What do you suppose Mr. Sillerton Jackson said about me the other day, mamma? He told Lanning I'd be considered extremely stylish in Paris. Didn't I tell you everyone likes my hair better, done like this, than plastered down—

CHARLOTTE

[*Interrupting.*]

Tina, Tina, why must you always think that people are interested in you?

TINA

[*Challengingly.*]

Why shouldn't I? Aren't they?

DELIA

[*Indulgently.*]

My dear! What will people think of you if you talk like that?

CHARLOTTE

[*Gravely; busy with her knitting again.*]

Just what she deserves, probably.

TINA

[*Springing up angrily.*]

Do tell Cousin Charlotte to stop finding fault with
me, mamma!

DELIA

[*Quickly, reprovingly.*]
Child, child—

CHARLOTTE

[*In the same grave voice, not lookng up
from her knitting.*]
Somebody must find fault, sometimes.

TINA

You see!

[*To* CHARLOTTE, *angrily.*]
You think mamma spoils me, but she doesn't! It's
just that *she* understands me—while you don't.
Mamma knows what it is to be young and have
everyone fond of her—while you—

[CHARLOTTE *rises abruptly.*]

CHARLOTTE

I must see that what's left of that Madeira doesn't
find its way to the kitchen.

[*She goes out quickly through the doorway
at the back, closing the door behind her.*]

DELIA

[*Deeply agitated; in a guarded voice.*]
I don't want you ever to speak to Cousin Chatty like
that again!

TINA

[*Sulking prettily, again settling herself on
the arm of* DELIA's *chair.*]

Mr. Sillerton Jackson told Lanning you were lucky
to have such a child—now that Dee's married, and
you'd be left all alone with just Cousin Chatty in the
house, if it weren't for me.

DELIA

[*Relenting; tenderly.*]

Of course I'm lucky. I know that . . . Cousin Chatty
and I are both lucky to have you.

TINA

[*With her arms about* DELIA'S *neck.*]

And even if I'm not your very own, like Dee, I feel
as if I were. And I can never thank you enough for
taking me in and treating me as if I were.

DELIA

[*Sharing the credit, half-heartedly.*]

Cousin Chatty wouldn't have come to live with me
after Dee's father died, unless I'd have you too.

TINA

[*Teasingly.*]

That's well enough to say, but would you have
wanted her without me? Tell the truth, mamma!

DELIA

I wanted you both. Now run and put on your cloak—

TINA

[*Rising.*]

I'm going—

> [*At that instant the door at the back opens
> and* DEE, LANNING *and* JOHN *enter,
> wearing their wraps.*]

DEE

[*Calmly.*]

I knew Tina would make us wait, so I brought her cloak down to her.

TINA

I was just going, but thanks—

> [LANNING *takes the cloak, and holds it for* TINA.]

DEE

[*Kissing* DELIA.]

Good-night, mamma.

DELIA

[*With a careless, affectionate kiss.*]

Good-night, my dear.

> [DEE *goes.*]

JOHN

[*Also kissing* DELIA *on each cheek.*]

Good-night; please say good-night to Cousin Chatty for us.

DELIA

I will.

> [JOHN *follows* DEE *into the passage.*]

TINA

I have my key, mamma; so please make Cousin Chatty go to bed. If I'm the least little bit late she's waiting up—pretending she didn't know whether I could get in or not.

> [LANNING *laughs.* DELIA *frowns a little.*

There is the sound of the outer door being opened.]

LANNING

[*A little self-consciously; feeling that he should not have laughed.*]

Good-night, Mrs. Ralston.

DELIA

Good-night, Lanning. How cold that wind is—!

[*Then to* TINA, *detaining her as* LANNING *goes.*]

Your boots! You haven't your boots, and there's snow on the ground.

TINA

I shan't need them. It's frozen dry; and it's only a step to the carriage.

DELIA

[*Reluctantly.*]

Then run on. Don't keep the door open.

TINA

Tell me, first—do I look nice, mamma?

DELIA

Lovely.

[TINA'S *answer is a pleased laugh and another kiss, then she runs out.*

DELIA *follows, standing in the passage to wave another good-bye. Then the outside door is closed, and* DELIA *comes back, idly, into the room. After an instant, however, she takes her embroidery from*

*a drawer of the table, and seating herself
in the zone of light from the lamp, busies
herself with her needle.* CHARLOTTE *returns presently; and drops into her chair
on the other side of the table, nearer the
fire. She picks up her knitting and begins
where she has left off. Suddenly she
breaks the silence which is heavy between them.*]

CHARLOTTE

[*Abruptly, not looking up.*]

I suppose you felt you had to scold Tina because of
the way she spoke to me.

DELIA

[*Her eyes on her embroidery.*]

I made her realize that it was disrespectful.

CHARLOTTE

[*Still not looking up.*]

She thinks I can't understand her because she con-
siders me an old maid—

DELIA

[*Lifting her head; pityingly.*]

Oh Chatty—!

CHARLOTTE

[*Still not looking up.*]

A ridiculous, narrow-minded old maid . . . What else
can she ever think me?

DELIA

My dear!

CHARLOTTE

[*Meeting* DELIA'S *eyes, at last; defensively.*]

Oh, but you needn't pity me. She's really mine.

[*Then, very simply.*]

I do scold her. But I don't want to be hard on her. As it is, I always practice what I'm going to say to her, if it's anything important, so I'll sound like an old maid cousin talking; not a mother.

[*Again she gives her entire attention to her knitting. Then again she speaks suddenly:*]

If you don't mind, I'd like to move down into the small bedroom Tina had before Delia's marriage, now that she's moved into Dee's room next to it.

DELIA

[*With some hesitation.*]

Of course I don't mind; but you'll be much less comfortable there than in your big room over mine. Unless it's on account of the stairs?

CHARLOTTE

[*Bluntly.*]

No; it's not the stairs. I'm not that old. It's because I should like to be next to Tina.

DELIA

[*Tactfully.*]

Very well; as you please. But I had meant to surprise Tina by doing her old room up as a boudoir where she could have books and things and see her friends.

CHARLOTTE

[*Again bluntly.*]

You're more than kind, Delia; but Tina mustn't have a boudoir.

DELIA

Then I'll give up the idea.

[*Again they are silent; then again* CHAR-
LOTTE *lifts her head from her work and
speaks in a troubled voice:*]

CHARLOTTE

You see that Tina has changed, don't you?

DELIA

[*Surprised; looking up.*]

Changed? Since when? How?

CHARLOTTE

Since Lanning Halsey has been coming here so often.

DELIA

[*Disturbed.*]

But it's very natural for him to come often, since his cousin is married to Dee. Still ... if you think it's because of Tina ... We must face the idea.

CHARLOTTE

[*Somberly.*]

I *do* face it.

DELIA

[*Arrested by* CHARLOTTE'S *tone.*]

And you dislike him? I mean as a husband for Tina?

CHARLOTTE

[*Still somberly.*]

Tina cannot afford to pick and choose.

DELIA

[*Slowly.*]

But there's nothing against Lanning, is there? Except that he seems uncertain as to his choice of a profession.

CHARLOTTE

[*Evenly.*]

Uncertainty about a profession may cause uncertainty about other things.

DELIA

[*Laying her embroidery on the table.*]

I don't understand you, Chatty.

CHARLOTTE

Haven't you heard that he thinks of studying architecture in Paris?

[*Their glances clash.*]

DELIA

[*Uncomfortably; quickly.*]

No. I heard only that he was thinking of traveling for a year. But if he's also thinking of asking Tina to marry him—

CHARLOTTE

[*Interrupting, sharply.*]

He's *not* thinking of asking Tina to marry him.

How could he? He earns nothing; and his allowance will be stopped if he marries against his parents' wishes.

DELIA

[*Trying to think of some answer.*]

But—

CHARLOTTE

[*Continuing evenly.*]

Unfortunately, my girl has no fortune and no name; and every careful mother we know has warned her sons against becoming interested.

DELIA

But after all, Tina's happy with us. She doesn't need to marry anyone.

CHARLOTTE

[*Passionately; rising abruptly.*]

Tina an old maid! Never! My child shall have her life.

DELIA

But she's not yet twenty. Wait.

CHARLOTTE

Wait? But if *she* doesn't wait?

DELIA

[*Angry and frightened.*]

Charlotte! Do you know what you're insinuating?

CHARLOTTE

Yes, I know.

DELIA

But it's too outrageous. No girl who is decent—

[*She halts suddenly, confused.*]

CHARLOTTE
[*Coolly.*]
Even nice girls are not always what you call decent.

DELIA
[*Picking up her tambour frame again, and trying to speak casually, as she pretends to give her attention to her embroidery.*]
I can't imagine what is to be gained by saying such things—even by thinking them. Surely you trust your own child.

CHARLOTTE
[*With a short laugh.*]
My mother trusted me.
[*Then, in a more matter of fact tone as she rises, puts her knitting away, and turns out the light in the lamps on the other side of the room.*]
But you look tired. I was forgetting that you had one of your headaches last night and didn't sleep. You must go to bed early. I don't want to keep you sitting up for my foolish girl.

DELIA
But why should you sit up for her, either? She has the key, and Dee is to bring her home.
[*She puts her embroidery away.*]

CHARLOTTE

[*Moving the chairs into order as she answers.*]

Yes, as you say, why should anyone sit up for Tina?

> [DELIA *goes and stands staring down into the fire, uneasily, while* CHARLOTTE *turns out the other lamps and lights their bedroom candles; she gives one to* DELIA, *and stands with the other in her hand, musing a moment, in the dark room, her figure stiffly outlined against the red glow from the fire.*]

When I was a girl, and lived with Grandmamma Lovell, I would have been very annoyed, I know, if anyone had sat up for me. But no one ever did . . . I was there, today. At Grandmamma's.

> [*She pauses, then continues after an instant:*]

The drawing-room is just as it used to be, though they've swathed the chandelier and draped sheets over the hard Empire sofa—now that she no longer comes downstairs . . . But those marble figures without any eyes are exactly where they always were on the mantel . . . and the carpet with its swans and garlands . . .

> [*She breaks off abruptly; then continues in a different voice, hurried and practical.*]

Don't wait for me. I'd forgotten the lamps in the other room. I hope they've kept your fire up.

DELIA

[*Tonelessly; not moving.*]
I'm sure they have.

CHARLOTTE

There's the medicine Dr. Lanskell left on the table. Take some if you can't sleep.

DELIA

[*Moving away from the mantel at last.*]
Thanks, I will.

[*She picks up the pill-box from the table, and then, with her candle in her other hand, moves towards* CHARLOTTE. *They meet in the center of the room.*]

DELIA

Good-night.

CHARLOTTE

[*Still with her candle in her hand.*]
Good-night.

[*They kiss each other formally; first on one cheek, then on the other. Then* DELIA *goes into the softly lighted passage, and disappears up the stairs.*

CHARLOTTE *watches until she is out of sight; then she closes the doors softly, and returns to her chair by the fire, setting her candle on the table beside her. After an instant she speaks—"practic-*

ing" what she is going to say to TINA
if she is late.]

CHARLOTTE

[*As she imagines an old maid relative
should speak.*]

What, Tina? You *walked* home with Lanning? You
imprudent child—in this wet snow! And without
your boots, too. You shouldn't do these things ...
You were always a delicate child ... Do you know
how late it is? I sat up because I couldn't for the
life of me remember if you'd taken your latch-key.
But don't tell your mamma, or she'll scold me for
growing forgetful, and sitting here in the cold. But
I've really been very comfortable—in fact I was
beginning to be afraid I'd slept instead of dozed
on the sofa—and missed hearing you come in—

[*As she talks the curtain falls slowly, to
rise again after a dark pause denoting
the passage of several hours.* CHARLOTTE
*is still in her chair, dozing lightly; but
the fire is only a red glow and her candle
has burned low.*

*Suddenly she is roused by the opening and
closing of the outer door. She rises,
snatches up her candle and looks at the
clock. For an instant she hesitates, and
then, in a panic of uncertainty, steals on
tip-toe, into the room at the right, softly
closing the door after her. Almost in-*

*stantly the door at the back is opened,
and* TINA *enters, followed by* LANNING.
*He looks at her, laughs, and deliberately
closes the door again.*]

TINA

[*Uneasily.*]

'Ssh! You must go.

LANNING

Not yet . . . No one's about.

[*He comes and catches her in his arms.*]

TINA

This is very wicked of us.

LANNING

Is it? Why?

TINA

[*Breathlessly.*]

You're going away—to Europe—

LANNING

I wish you were coming with me.

TINA

I wish you wouldn't go.

LANNING

You don't think I *want* to go?

TINA

Then why do you go?

LANNING

I'm no good here. You know that. I'm not worth
my salt in any regular business. If I were, things
might be different.

TINA

[*Shyly.*]

What sort of things, Lanning?

LANNING

With us, darling ...

> [*She jerks herself from his arms and goes
> towards the fireplace.* LANNING *follows
> her.*]

Cold?

> [*He again tries to put his arms about her,
> but again she moves away, and stands
> against the chair nearest the fire.*]

TINA

[*Shivering; moodily.*]

No ... yes ... I don't know ...

LANNING

[*Taking her by the arms.*]

Goose! Don't be angry with me. You know I can't
marry anyone, yet ... You're shivering. I shouldn't
have made you wait until the carriages were all gone.
Sit down. Let me see if your feet are wet.

> [*She sits, as he commands. He drops on
> his knees, crying out, contritely.*]

Heavens, Tina! You shouldn't have walked in these
things. Why didn't you tell me?

TINA

[*In a very little voice.*]

I loved it—the snow—and the moonlight—and the

icy trees in the Square—and being with you—at last—all alone. What are you doing?

LANNING

Taking off your wet slippers and stockings. I loved it, too; but I should have taken better care of you, just the same.

TINA

[*Trying to draw away her foot.*]
Don't—!

LANNING

[*Gaily, tenderly.*]
Be still, little foot! Why are you running away when I'm trying to make you all warm again?

TINA

Silly!

LANNING

[*Setting her bare foot on his knee.*]
Now for the other little foot; both little feet have to be warm—or little Tina—

[*He strips the other foot of its stocking, holds it in his hand, and looks up at her with sudden alarm.*]
Oh, Tina—what if you *should* die! You won't, will you—while I'm away? Promise not to.

TINA

[*Leaning forward and catching his face in her hands; simply.*]
I shall want to. Because you've gone.

LANNING

Dearest—!

> [*He lifts his face; she bends hers; they kiss. Then she draws back, and his head falls on her knees.*]

TINA

> [*Gravely.*]

That's the first time; and I shall never kiss anyone but you—ever—

LANNING

I've no right, but—

> [*Again he lifts his face, and again she bends hers to his lips. The door at the back opens and DELIA enters; she carries her candle, and her hair ripples about her face; she wears a dressing-gown.*]

DELIA

> [*Sharply.*]

Tina!

TINA

> [*In a muffled voice.*]

Mamma—!

DELIA

> [*Trying not to look at them; deeply embarrassed and uneasy.*]

I've not been able to sleep. I heard you come in. It's late—

TINA

[*In the same muffled voice, as* LANNING *gets to his feet.*]

I know; I'm sorry.

DELIA

[*Trying to be stern.*]

Go to bed, now. Lanning.

LANNING

[*In a low voice.*]

Yes, Mrs. Ralston?

DELIA

[*Awkwardly.*]

Good-night.

LANNING

Good-night.

[*Then to* TINA.]

Good-night, Tina.

TINA

[*Very low.*]

Good-night, Lanning.

[*He goes towards the door at the back.*]

LANNING

[*To* DELIA, *as she stands aside to let him pass.*]

It's ever so nice of you not to scold me for being here, Mrs. Ralston.

[CHARLOTTE *has heard as she opens the door at the right; she comes forward*

*trembling with anger, still holding her
candle in her shaking hand.*]

CHARLOTTE

Yes; don't scold *him*. This is Tina's fault, not his.
Any boy would do the same if she permitted it!

LANNING

[*Turning.*]

It's not *her* fault!

CHARLOTTE

[*With a short laugh.*]

No? Well, no matter who's to blame this time, it's
not to happen again. I hope you both understand
that!

LANNING

But, Miss Chatty—

CHARLOTTE

[*To* DELIA, *not letting him speak.*]

Tell him not to come here again! It's your house or
I'd tell him myself.

LANNING

[*Angrily.*]

Oh, very well, if you and Mrs. Ralston don't want
me—

TINA

[*Rising from the chair where she has been
huddling.*]

Tell Cousin Chatty to take that back, mamma! Tell
Lanning he's to come when he wants to! Tell him,
mamma! It *is* your house, not hers!

LANNING

[*Coolly, after waiting an instant for* DELIA
to speak as she fails to do so.]

Don't bother, Mrs. Ralston. I'm sailing soon: next
week, probably—so it doesn't matter very much
whether I'm forbidden this door or not. I'd only
have come again to say good-bye, in any case.

TINA

[*With a cry.*]

Good-bye!

LANNING

Yes; that's the only thing I can say, in the circum-
stances, it seems. I'm sorry I've made Miss Chatty
so angry with you, but—

[*Turning to* DELIA *and* CHARLOTTE,
speaking defiantly, and a little grandly.]

—it didn't seem a crime to *me,* for Tina to stay on
after John and Delia left without her ... It didn't
even seem a crime to come in with her, and see that
she took off her wet shoes. I warmed her feet with
my hands—and *that* didn't seem a crime, either;
but I apologize, if you think it was a liberty. As I
said before, it wasn't her fault, and I hope she'll
not be made to suffer for it. Also, as I said before,
it can't happen again. Good-night ... And good-bye,
Tina.

[*He goes, closing the door after him.*]

TINA

[*Desperately.*]

Lanning—wait!

[*Then, as there is no answer, sobbing, stormily.*]

You see! You see what she's done, mamma! She's driven Lanning away!

CHARLOTTE

Oh, no—my child—*I've* not driven him away! If he's not coming here again it's because he'd find it awkward when he has no intention of marrying a girl who's so free with her kisses.

TINA

[*At white heat.*]

That's not true; that's not true!

CHARLOTTE

[*Somberly.*]

You know it's true. I don't know all he said to you —I didn't want to hear—but you don't think for a minute that anything *I* could say *would* drive him away if he really cared for you, do you?

DELIA

[*Trying to stand between them.*]

Your cousin is right, Tina. If Lanning goes it's because he doesn't care as much for you as you think—

TINA

[*Bitterly, sobbing again.*]

But he would have cared, if she'd not driven him

away! I'd have *made* him care. Now I can't! Now he's gone—and I'll never forgive her—never—!

DELIA

Tina!

TINA

I won't!

[*To* CHARLOTTE.]

You'd no business to meddle! And if you ever do it again I'll never speak to you as long as I live!

DELIA

[*Sharply.*]

Go to your room, Tina!

TINA

[*Crying.*]

I'm going, mamma, but before I do, she's got to know that I'm sick of her fault-finding and her spying and her meddling! *You* can say what you please to me, because you understand me, and I love you; but she's only a sour old maid who hates me because I'm young—and attractive—and alive; while she's old and hideous and dried up—and has never known anything about love! I won't have her interfering with my life, I tell you! I won't have it!

DELIA

Tina—Tina!

[*She drops down into a chair as if unable to stand, and covers her face with her hands. Instantly* TINA *is frightened and sobered.*]

TINA

[*Kneeling beside her.*]

Mamma! I'm sorry, mamma! Don't cry—

[DELIA *points towards the stairs.* TINA *understands.*]

I'm going . . .

[*Then frightened by what she has said, she slips past* CHARLOTTE, *who stands as rigid as a statue, towards the door. There she turns, speaking humbly.*]

You'll come in and say good-night to me, won't you, mamma? Please . . .

[*But* DELIA *only answers with a little gesture of dismissal, and* TINA *goes, closing the door after her . . .* CHARLOTTE *moves to the sofa, at last, and sits down.*]

DELIA

[*As soon as she is able to speak.*]

Poor Chatty! I'm so sorry.

CHARLOTTE

[*Somberly.*]

This has gone on long enough. I see my mistake now, and I mean to remedy it.

DELIA

Your mistake?

CHARLOTTE

You've been good to us. But I understand my duty now. We must go.

DELIA

What?

CHARLOTTE

Don't think me ungrateful. You've done all you could for us both. But my eyes are open now. If I am to save my child, I must take her away.

DELIA

Take her away? Charlotte, in God's name, what *are* you saying?

CHARLOTTE

I must take Tina away. We must go somewhere where we're not known—where we shall live among plain people, leading plain lives. Somewhere, where they've never heard of the hundred-dollar baby—where she can find herself a husband and make herself a home.

DELIA

[*Unbelievingly.*]
You'd take Tina away from me now!

CHARLOTTE

[*Repeating.*]
I'm not ungrateful—

DELIA

[*Desperately.*]
Oh, don't let's speak of gratitude! What does it matter whether you're grateful or not? It's Tina I'm thinking of—

CHARLOTTE

[*As she rises and crosses the room towards* DELIA.]

Of course it's Tina you're thinking of—Tina and Clem Spender!

DELIA

You're insane, Charlotte! I've not thought of Clement Spender for years!

CHARLOTTE

[*Losing all self-control.*]

Oh, but you have! You have! You've thought of him in thinking of Tina! Of him, and nobody else. Everything you've done—*for me*—was for him!

DELIA

Upon my honor, I have *not* thought of him!

CHARLOTTE

[*Her voice rising to a scream.*]

You've thought of him whether you knew it or not. A woman never stops thinking of the man she loves. She thinks of him years afterwards in all sorts of unconscious ways, in thinking of all sorts of things—a sunset, an old song, a cameo on a chain—!

[*Then she breaks off with a short laugh, and her voice drops to a whisper as she continues:*]

I know. I've thought of him too. Only tonight it wasn't Tina and Lanning Halsey here—it wasn't those two I saw from the window—sauntering through the icy weather—like lovers in a midsummer

glade, not feeling the wind and the cold at all. I saw
us—long ago—walking home to a darkened house—
on just such a night . . . when I didn't know whether
there was snow beneath my feet—or daisies . . .

    [*Then harshly.*]

I suppose you found them in each other's arms. I was
afraid to come in—afraid I'd see *us!*

DELIA

Hush, hush—you mustn't say these things! You
mustn't think them!

CHARLOTTE

    [*Triumphantly.*]

Ah—you can't forgive me because Clem Spender
didn't quite break his heart over you! That's why you
like keeping me at your mercy—and taking his child
from me! That's why you took us in—to give *his*
child a home.

DELIA

    [*Suddenly losing all patience; at white
      heat.*]

And suppose that's all true! Suppose I couldn't leave
Clem Spender's child to the mercy of chance? She's
yours too. And to take her away now—from the life
you made such a sacrifice to give her—would be too
cruel. Too cruel—to her! Even more cruel to her
than to me.

CHARLOTTE

    [*Faltering a little; impressed against her
      will by what* DELIA *has just said.*]

My mind's made up. I know what is best for my own child.

CHARLOTTE

DELIA

Is destroying her happiness best?

CHARLOTTE

What's ahead for her, here? For a girl without a name or a penny, among cautious people like the Halseys and their kind? You've done all you could for her. But you see what's come of it, so far. Now—

DELIA

No, I've not done *all* I could. But I'm going to, now, if you'll let me.

[*As* CHARLOTTE *looks at her quickly, blankly, she continues:*]

I will adopt Tina, legally.

CHARLOTTE

Adopt her? Adopt *Tina?* You!

DELIA

Oh, you needn't think the idea hasn't occurred to me before! It has, from time to time—ever since the two of you first came to live with me and she began calling me "mamma" because Dee did.

CHARLOTTE

[*Soberly.*]

You've never mentioned it before.

DELIA

No. Because I wasn't sure how you'd take it.

CHARLOTTE

[*Drily.*]

Perhaps you weren't sure how others would take it—
your own child, for instance.

DELIA

That's true; I wasn't. But now I realize that if Tina
is to be happy, her position must be made unassail-
able; both financially and socially, and this is the only
way I know of doing it.

CHARLOTTE

[*Still hostile.*]

It isn't clear to me that your adopting Tina would
help so much.

DELIA

You mean you don't see what a difference it will
make if I give her my name—the Ralston name, and
my money—the money my mother left me? My own
child has all she'll ever need from her father—

CHARLOTTE

[*Cutting her short.*]

No, no! I refuse.

DELIA

You refuse? You dare to sacrifice Tina's happiness
to your pride?

CHARLOTTE

[*Bitterly.*]

My *pride!*

[*Then brokenly.*]

My pride . . . What pride have I, except in my child?
And that I'll never sacrifice. No, no—it's gone on

long enough—this—this mistake! I'm going to take
her away.

DELIA

[*Desperately.*]

You are going to sacrifice her, then? Sacrifice her to
your desire for mastery! When she might have everything she wants, and you say you want for her—even
Lanning Halsey for a husband; a home of her own.

> [CHARLOTTE *bends her head suddenly, and
> covers her face with her hands.* DELIA *is
> quick with her advantage; continuing:*]

It's as she said; he will love her if she wants him to.
She can make him love her, if there's no reason why
he shouldn't. And if she has money of her own, and
my name, the Halseys won't find her such a bad
match for their son after all . . . Give her this chance!
What mother wouldn't? And if Lanning takes her
away from us both, in time, it won't be like really
giving her up. Couldn't we just go on loving her together?

> [*She has dropped down upon the sofa, be-
> side* CHARLOTTE, *and put an arm about
> her shoulder. Suddenly* CHARLOTTE'S
> *rigid attitude relaxes, and she reaches
> for* DELIA'S *hand and lifts it to her
> cheek.*]
>
> *During the instant of silence between them
> which follows, the door at the back is
> opened by* TINA, *who stands on the*

*threshold in a dressing-gown. She speaks
uncertainly:*]

TINA

Mamma, aren't you coming up? I've been waiting
for you.

CHARLOTTE

[*In a flat voice, motioning* DELIA *away.*]
Go on up with her ... I'll come presently ... Good-
night.

[*Without a word* DELIA *rises, and takes
her candle from the table; then she joins*
TINA *in the doorway and the two disappear up the stairs;* CHARLOTTE *watches
them without moving as the curtain
falls.*]

FIFTH EPISODE
. 1854

An evening the following June.

The same room, which again looks different because it has been transformed into a chapel for a wedding. The lace-trimmed, flower-decked altar hides the fireplace, and lilies and dwarf-orange trees are arranged on each side of the doorway at the back. The long windows at the right stand open letting in the moonlight and a soft breeze which now and then drives a few fallen flower petals across the floor. Most of the furniture has been taken out, and the sofa and few chairs which remain have been pushed about any way; while groups of small gilt chairs, unplaced, stand here and there, where they are not too much in the way, and are stacked upside down, one on top of another, in the passage beyond the open doorway. The lamps have been removed with the tables; but every gas-jet is lighted, even the dozens in the crystal chandelier; so the room is startlingly bright.

LANNING, DEE *and* JOHN *are standing about;* MRS. MINGOTT *sits on the oddly awry rosewood sofa;*

DELIA *looking both tired and happy in a big chair near the window;* DR. LANSKELL *sits beside* MRS. MINGOTT; *and* TINA *is everywhere.*

TINA

[*Gesturing as she talks.*]

And as soon as the wedding march begins, Lanning will come through that door and then I'll come through this one—with Dee going in front, and mamma to give me away—

[*She stops abruptly, and darts to where DELIA sits, to kiss her.*]

Darling mamma—!

MRS. MINGOTT

[*With a sharp glance at TINA; to LANNING.*]

She's too happy, Lanning. When she talks she laughs; when she walks she dances; she sings and she runs about, flinging her happiness in all our faces until I'm afraid for her.

DELIA

[*Quickly.*]

Don't say that, Aunt Carrie—don't think such things.

MRS. MINGOTT

All the same, I am.

TINA

[*Rising on her toes with a dancer's movement, because she cannot keep still, her*

*laughter and her arms fluttering up-
wards.*]
But *I'm* not! Nothing can happen now!

MRS. MINGOTT

[*Looking from* TINA *to* LANNING.]
Listen to her! Well, let us hope nothing does keep
the two of you from that altar tomorrow.

LANNING

Nothing could—

MRS. MINGOTT

'Ssh, children! . . . A dozen things *could* happen—
[*Then generously.*]
But they won't.

[CHARLOTTE *appears suddenly in the doorway at the back, and stands looking
about. She is a grim figure in the pleasant scene, in her dark dress and black
apron; and when she speaks abruptly, it
is with a kind of dull, impersonal satisfaction, and to no one in particular.*]

CHARLOTTE

Everything's done that can be done tonight. I've been
to the kitchen to have the lemon and orange peeling
mixed with sugar and bitters for the punch. And I've
told Melissa Grimes she'd better count on two hundred plates of ice cream. Two hundred? Yes, I suppose she had, with all the Philadelphia connections
coming.

MRS. MINGOTT

There's nothing more tiring than the hurly-burly just before a wedding.

CHARLOTTE

[*Moving forward and picking up flower petals she sees on the floor.*]

The floor will have to be swept and the chairs put in place after they've finished with the flowers in the morning ... I've decided to give the clergymen that little study to change their robes in.

[*Then straightening up, and looking round.*]

I can't think of anything else.

[*But she moves to the doorway and rearranges the flowers in their vases, as* MRS. MINGOTT *resumes.*]

MRS. MINGOTT

And a house-wedding always makes a great to-do. I don't approve of them, myself. Leave them to the Methodists and the Baptists, and other altarless sects.

[*Then to* DELIA, *modifying her disapproval.*]

Though a great many people prefer them, of course. You were married at home, I remember. And I kissed you and Jim under the bell of white roses in the hall.

DELIA

[*Startled.*]

I was just thinking of my own wedding—

CHARLOTTE

[*Looking round; tonelessly.*]

So was I.

[*She comes forward and drops down on a
small, straight chair. Her hands look
curiously idle, lying empty in her lap.*]

MRS. MINGOTT

[*With one of her rare sentimentalities.*]

How many weddings I've come back from Paris for,
in my time!

[*Then she rises.*]

I think I'll go up now.

[*To* TINA.]

Come and kiss me good-night, my dear.

TINA

Good-night, Aunt Carrie—

LANNING

[*Kissing her hand.*]

Good-night, Mrs. Mingott.

MRS. MINGOTT

Good-night, Lanning.

DEE

I'll go up with you, Aunt Carrie—

MRS. MINGOTT

You needn't.

DEE

I want to.

JOHN

We'll both go.

DELIA

Good-night, Aunt Carrie. Sleep well—

MRS. MINGOTT

I always sleep well.

> [*With a nod to the others.*]

Good-night.

> [*She goes into the passage, with* DEE *on one side and* JOHN *on the other; but at the foot of the stairs she dismisses them.*]

MRS. MINGOTT

Run along and take a walk in the moonlight, children. I can still manage the stairs without an arm.

> [*Then she turns her back on them and goes up the steps with astonishing sprightliness, while* JOHN *and* DEE *take her suggestion and disappear from the passage in the opposite direction on their way into the moonlight.*]

CHARLOTTE

> [*Abruptly.*]

The bride's the one who should be sent to bed. Say good-night to Lanning, too, Tina.

> [*Then to* DELIA.]

She's tired.

DELIA

> [*Reluctantly.*]

Yes, Tina, you should go to bed now—

TINA

But I'm not sleepy, mamma—

CHARLOTTE

You can rest, whether you sleep or not.

DELIA

[*Echoing her.*]

Yes—you should go up now—

DR. LANSKELL

Lanning will have a pleasant sail in the moonlight. There's just enough breeze to take his cat-boat up the river at a good clip. If he waits it may die down.

LANNING

I'm going. Come across the park with me, Tina—

CHARLOTTE

Not tonight, Tina.

DELIA

No; it's late. Say good-night to her here, Lanning.

LANNING

Then good-night; good-night, Miss Chatty; good-night, sir—

DR. LANSKELL *and* DELIA

[*Together.*]

Good-night, my dear—

Good-night, my boy—

TINA

[*As she slips her arm through his.*]

Only as far as the steps, mamma—

[*Before even* CHARLOTTE *can protest, they have disappeared through the open win-*

*dow, on to the verandah. As their laugh-
ter floats back,* DELIA *turns to* CHAR-
LOTTE, *who has been standing since*
MRS. MINGOTT *said good-night.*]

DELIA

You must be tired, too; do sit down again, dear, and
rest—

CHARLOTTE

[*Interrupting, as if unconscious of what*
DELIA *has been saying.*]

The doilies! I must see if Aunt Cecilia Vandergrave
sent hers, as she promised. They may have been taken
upstairs with the presents.

DELIA

[*Helplessly.*]

Doilies? Haven't we enough?

CHARLOTTE

With hers we shall manage beautifully.

[*Then she hurries from the room, through
the door at the back, and runs up the
stairs.*]

DELIA

[*To* DR. LANSKELL; *in a low, intimate
voice, as they seat themselves near one
another.*]

I think poor Chatty is really happy at last.

DR. LANSKELL

[*Drily.*]

Why?

DELIA

She came into my room this morning to talk about
something unimportant; then she said suddenly,
"We're giving her up, I know, but now at least she'll
never suspect the truth."

DR. LANSKELL

And you judge she's happy from *that?*

DELIA

At least, she's relieved . . . I think she's been afraid
all these years that she might tell Tina some time,
herself.

DR. LANSKELL

[*Incredulously.*]

But why on earth should you think a thing like that?

DELIA

[*With a certain reservation in her tone.*]

I have my reasons. Chatty isn't always herself when
she loses her head. And if she ever *had* said anything
to Tina—

DR. LANSKELL

[*As* DELIA *pauses.*]

You think it would have broken the child's heart, I
suppose?

DELIA

It would have done no good. . .

DR. LANSKELL

The poor woman. . .

DELIA

'Ssh—

[*She sees* TINA *as she returns from the verandah.*]

TINA

He's gone . . . I'll go up now.

DELIA

Yes, do, darling.

TINA

Will you come up and say good-night to me, mamma?

DELIA

Of course.

TINA

Because tonight . . .

> [*Dreamily, leaning her face against* DELIA, *from back of her chair.*]

. . . it's as Aunt Carrie said.

> [*She halts, then adds, prettily:*]

I *am* much too happy, mamma. And I'm just a little afraid, though I pretended I wasn't. Lanning says we've all been straws whirling about on a sunlit torrent, ever since mamma adopted me, Dr. Lanskell, and his parents decided he might get married, whether he had a profession or not . . . They've been sweet to me, but if mamma hadn't cared enough for me to give me her name and the money, they'd not have wanted him to care either.

DELIA

Nonsense, darling.

TINA

Oh, I *know,* mamma. . . I know what I owe you. I owe you everything.

> [CHARLOTTE, *coming down the stairs with the doilies in her hand, pauses to listen; first because it is a pleasure to hear* TINA'S *happy voice, and then because what she says touches her closely.*]

TINA

> [*Continuing.*]

Everything—even Lanning; and I'm glad.

> [*Looking at* DR. LANSKELL, *with her arms still about* DELIA'S *neck.*]

I used to wonder who I really was; but I don't care now. I'd rather have *her* for my mamma than anyone in the world.

DELIA

> [*Both pleased and a little embarrassed.*]

Well, the lawyers have done everything they could to make you my daughter, haven't they?

TINA

> [*Playing with* DELIA'S *hair.*]

Dee doesn't love her as much as I do, and she doesn't love Dee as much as she loves me.

DELIA

> [*Not really displeased by* TINA'S *assurance.*]

Tina, Tina, you mustn't say such things!

> [CHARLOTTE *comes down the stairs, mov-*

*ing very softly, and rounding the newel
post, turns in the direction of the back of
the house, but not before she has heard
more that is very painful for her to
listen to.*]

TINA

Well, even Cousin Chatty said you didn't take half so
much interest in Dee's wedding as you have in mine.
She said you ordered twelve dozen of everything for
her, and let it go at that, but nothing was good
enough for me!

DELIA

Your Cousin Chatty has been just as much interested
as I've been. And just as generous to you.

TINA

[*Soberly, as if reminded of a surprising
fact.*]

Yes, what do you think, Dr. Lanskell? Cousin Chatty
gave me all her grandmother's jewels.

DR. LANSKELL

I think you're a lucky girl. I've seen them.

TINA

I know I am. And my wedding veil. She wanted me
to wear the wedding dress that she was going to wear
once, too, and didn't; but I told her I wanted to wear
mamma's—the one Dee wore last June. It's India
mull, and I knew mamma wanted me to, though she
wouldn't say so. It seems odd to think that anyone
ever wanted to marry Cousin Chatty.

[*She laughs a little and then yawns.* CHAR-
LOTTE *is gone.*]

DELIA
[*Reaching up and touching* TINA'S *cheek.*]
There, you *are* tired, chatterbox.

TINA
All the same, I won't go to sleep till you've come in
and said good-night.

DELIA
I've told you I'd come. Now, run along.
[*But* TINA *has more to say to* DR. LANS-
KELL.]
TINA
[*Showing a cameo which she wears on a
chain.*]
Mamma gave me this; besides her other presents.
She's always worn it, and it's the very first thing I
remember in my life. A beautiful lady holding me
on her lap—and putting this around my neck, then
kissing me, and going away ... It's Psyche and
Eros.

DR. LANSKELL
It's very pretty.

TINA
I love it.
[*Then she puts out her hand, impulsively.*]
Good-night, Dr. Lanskell. You were always kind to
me, when I was little. I remember that, too.

[*Then, dropping a kiss on the top of*
DELIA'S *head, she adds:*]

Don't forget I'm waiting for you, mamma.

[*And with another laugh she disappears
through the doorway at the back, and
runs, singing softly, up the stairs.*]

DR. LANSKELL

I must go too, now.

[*But he continues without moving.*]

I suppose Chatty takes the child's happiness as the
direct result of your generosity.

DELIA

[*A little self-consciously.*]

She's not said so, but I've sensed her gratitude from
the night she made up her mind to let me adopt Tina.

[*Then quickly.*]

Oh, I know you thought I took too much on myself
when I kept Chatty from marrying Joe, that time.
I've not forgotten what you said about meddling with
another person's destiny.

DR. LANSKELL

[*Gently.*]

But I know what you've paid for your mistake—if it
was a mistake. Chatty's been jealous from that moment in her nursery when the child went to you, in-
stinctively, as to a mother. And no jealous woman
was ever easy to live with.

DELIA

[*Quietly.*]

Thank you for realizing that. And now that Tina's leaving us—

[*With a deep sigh.*]

—from tomorrow evening on, till death comes for one of us, we'll be sitting here alone together—beside the same lamp, in an empty house—with God knows what thoughts to keep us company. This—this isn't like me.

DR. LANSKELL

I know that. But perhaps it's because memories have a way of coming to the family feasts—whether they're invited or not. Good-night, my dear.

[*Both get up.*]

DELIA

Good-night. . . I'll go to the door with you.

> [*They pass through the doorway at the back, disappearing from sight in the direction of the front door.* CHARLOTTE *enters from the room at the right; her face is hard and set. She pauses on the threshold, seeing the room empty; then comes forward, and stands looking at the altar; motionless.*
>
> *Hearing* DELIA'S *step in the passage,* CHARLOTTE *turns quickly, in time to see her start up the stairs.*]

CHARLOTTE

[*Sharply.*]

Delia!

[DELIA *stops;* CHARLOTTE *moves towards her.*]

DELIA

Yes?

CHARLOTTE

[*With an undercurrent of anger and jealousy.*]

You're going up, now—to speak to Tina?

DELIA

Yes, unless there's something you want to talk to me about first . . . ?

[*Coming back into the room; then continuing, as* CHARLOTTE *faces her without answering.*]

I think before she goes to sleep I ought to—

CHARLOTTE

Yes; you think you ought to—

DELIA

[*Coming nearer, and lowering her voice slightly, feeling that she is discussing a delicate matter.*]

Well, you agree, don't you, that a word ought to be said to the child, before her marriage, as to her— her new duties and responsibilities? And tomorrow in the midst of all the excitement there'll be no opportunity; so I told her I'd go up to her—

CHARLOTTE

[*Interrupting; harshly.*]

I understand; but please understand me, too, if I ask you not to.

CHARLOTTE

DELIA

[*With an effort at patience.*]

I confess I don't understand you, Charlotte. You surely feel that on the night before her wedding a girl ought to have her mother's counsel.

CHARLOTTE

Naturally. That's why *I* must be the one to talk to Tina tonight. Just tonight *I* am her mother!

DELIA

Charlotte! *You're* not going to tell her that! Not now!

CHARLOTTE

[*With a short laugh.*]

Do you hate me for it as much as all that?

DELIA

Hate you? What a word to use between us!

CHARLOTTE

[*Somberly.*]

It's the word that's been between us since the beginning. You've hated me from the moment you knew I was the mother of Clem Spender's child. And there's been hate between us ever since. Because his child is mine instead of yours!

DELIA

[*Wearily.*]

Yes. I realize now that you believe I've hated you because you have hated me. Hated me in spite of everything I've tried to do for you.

CHARLOTTE

Nothing was for me—it was all for Clement Spender and his child!

DELIA

You said that once before. Well, suppose it was! Our lives are spent now; and so is Clement Spender's. But Tina's is ahead of her; and it seems to me that if you loved her as I love her you couldn't stand here, before her bridal altar, and talk of hatred. Not here, not in this room, where the very air is full of her happiness tonight! It's wicked of you, Charlotte! Wicked!

CHARLOTTE

No, that's not true! I'm not wicked. I wouldn't have done to you what you've done to me. From the beginning you've deliberately divided me from my daughter! Do you suppose it's been easy all these years to hear her call you *mother?* Oh, I know it was agreed between us that she must never guess! But you needn't have perpetually come between us! If you hadn't, she'd have had no one to turn to but me. She'd have had to love *me!* But for all your patience and generosity, you've ended by robbing me of my child. That's why I can talk of hatred here before this altar tonight! And that's why— before she's his tomorrow: tonight, just tonight,

she belongs to me! That's why I won't let her call
anyone else *mother* tonight!

DELIA

Very well; I won't go up to her; it's your right, not
mine. And if you want her to know the truth about
her birth, it's your right to tell her that, too. As you
say—I have intervened in your life—and it's natural
you should hate me for it. And that I should be
sorry. I've played my part, done my utmost—but I
realize now that all my efforts to insure the girl's
happiness have ended in failure—

> [*She breaks off, unable to say more, and
> sits down weakly, covering her face with
> her hands, to hide her sudden tears.*]

CHARLOTTE
> [*After watching her an instant with brood-
> ing eyes.*]

I suppose you imagine it will be a tragedy for Tina
—to learn that she's my daughter. Well—we shall
see.

> [*Then she turns and goes out through the
> doorway at the back, with a kind of omi-
> nous stateliness. Almost instantly* DELIA
> *rises, and starts towards the door as if
> to call her back. But she pauses, help-
> lessly.*
> DEE *appears in the open window from the
> verandah, a little bouquet in her hand.*]

DEE

[*As to a child, as she comes towards* DELIA.]

Are *you* still up—

DELIA

[*Turning quickly, with a wan smile.*]

You see—

[*She goes back to her chair and sits down.*]

DEE

And you were almost too tired at dinner to keep awake.

[*Then in a different voice.*]

I thought you'd gone up to Tina, of course.

DELIA

[*Echoing.*]

Gone up to Tina—?

DEE

[*Showing* DELIA *the bouquet as she sits on a stool beside her.*]

I've just gathered these for her. I've been thinking of last June, and the night before my wedding, and our talk together. And it came back to me how everything you said was . . . lovely . . . how it helped. I went to sleep certain that whatever might happen to any girl, love and marriage should be a part of it; and then—just as I was almost asleep, Tina knocked and came in, and gave me a bouquet—like this— that she'd just gathered for me. And she looked at me so oddly, and said, *"You'll* always be happy, Dee," in such a way that I knew she was afraid *she* might never be ... That's why I was glad you adopted her, mamma—although she's a flighty little thing in many ways. She was thinking of Lanning then. And it would have been unfair to have taken her in and then not have stood by her, the way you have— to the end; so she could be happy, too.

DELIA

[*A catch in her voice, looking at* DEE *with new eyes.*]

Thank you, my darling, for telling me this, *tonight.*

DEE

You see, I understand you, mamma ... You are a dear romantic goose. Will you give this to Tina for me when you go up—?

[*She puts the little bouquet into* DELIA's *hand, continuing, as she rises:*]

She'll understand ... And just talk to her the way you talked to me. A dear romantic goose is exactly the sort of person a girl wants to talk to the night before her wedding. Only you are really much more than that, dear—at times. At times no one's so wise ... Good-night.

[*She kisses* DELIA *lightly on the cheeks.*]

I'm going back to John. He's romantic too, tonight —and insists on wandering about in the moonlight— making plans for *his* son's wedding.

DELIA

What—?

DEE

[*With elaborate nonchalance.*]

Oh yes . . . You're going to be a grandmother, one of these days, after nearly a year of uncertainty.

[*She laughs.*]

DELIA

[*Rising and putting her arms about her.*]

My dear girl—my own dear girl—!

DEE

It's nothing to cry about—

DELIA

It's not that—

DEE

I know; it's everything . . . Now go up to Tina—and then to bed—like a good child.

[*She kisses* DELIA *again, laughing her sweet superior little laugh, and then goes to the window. There she calls: "Oo-ee," and* JOHN'S *voice calls back to her: "Oo-ee" . . . Then she is gone.* CHARLOTTE *enters and is standing near* DELIA *before* DELIA *sees her; there is something quite different in* CHARLOTTE'S *face; she looks at peace.*]

CHARLOTTE

Delia—

DELIA

Ah—!

CHARLOTTE

Tina's not asleep yet. There's a light under her door; but I didn't go in.

DELIA

What?

CHARLOTTE

[*In a matter-of-fact voice.*]

No. So she's still waiting for you.

DELIA

But—?

CHARLOTTE

I couldn't, after all ... *tell her,* I mean. If she's never really belonged to me, perhaps it's because her father never really belonged to me either. Both were yours. He loved you; so she loved you, too. So I—I decided to say nothing.

DELIA

[*Gently.*]

But you might have gone in and said good-night to her, dear. You might have had a talk together.

CHARLOTTE

I thought of that, too. I stood in the passage, and tried—

DELIA

Tried—?

CHARLOTTE

To think of something ... something to say to her without ... without her guessing.

[*Then she smiles, though her eyes are
wet.*]

But it's no use. There's nothing I *can* say. You're
the mother she wants. Go to her. It's not your fault
—or mine.

DELIA

Oh!

CHARLOTTE

After all, she was mine when she was little.

DELIA

Come with me, Charlotte. We'll go to her together—

CHARLOTTE

No—you—

[*Then she turns her back on* DELIA *and
goes out abruptly, through the window.
She has seen* TINA *in the doorway.*]

TINA

Mamma—

DELIA

[*As* CHARLOTTE *disappears without looking back.*]

What is it, Tina?

TINA

I've been waiting for you. You said you'd come up.

DELIA

[*With a singular flatness in her voice.*]

I know; but I've been talking to Dee. There was
something she wanted to tell me.

[*Then remembering the flowers in her
        hand.*]
She wanted you to have these.

TINA

Oh—she didn't forget that last year—

DELIA

No, she didn't forget. Tina—

TINA

[*Startled by a strange note in* DELIA'S
        voice.]
Yes, mamma?

DELIA

Do you want to do something that will make me very
happy?

TINA

Anything—you darling!

DELIA

[*Discouraging with her tone and a ges-
        ture* TINA'S *impulse to kiss her.*]
Then find your Cousin Charlotte. She's just gone
into the garden. And when you've found her, remember this; she didn't marry a man who loved her
very much, and who would have given her everything she wanted—because she wouldn't give you
up. That's why she is an old maid.

TINA

Oh—!

[*With just a hint of reproach in the question.*]

Why didn't anyone ever tell me that before?

DELIA

Sometimes people don't think; sometimes they are selfish. But remember—and try to make her glad of her choice tonight. Without telling her that I asked you to.

TINA

[*In a low miserable voice.*]

And I've always been so horrid . . .

> [*She starts towards the window, and stops, as* DELIA *puts out her hand.*]

DELIA

There's one thing more—

TINA

[*Turning.*]

Yes?

DELIA

When you go away tomorrow—at the very last moment, you understand—after you've said good-bye to me, and to everybody else—just as Lanning helps you into the carriage . . .

TINA

Yes?

DELIA

Lean down and give your last kiss to Cousin Charlotte. Don't forget—the very last.

TINA

I won't forget ... There she is now, at the end of
the walk.

[*Then calling from the window:*]
Cousin Charlotte—Cousin Charlotte—

[*She disappears, as the curtain falls.*]

(2)